MY PRECIOUS ABALONE

دار جامعة حمد بن خليفة للنشر
HAMAD BIN KHALIFA UNIVERSITY PRESS

Contents

DEDICATIONS 9
INTRODUCTION 11
I KNOW WHAT I WANT TO BE 17
A DIFFICULT START 25
DRAWING STRENGTH FROM OTHERS 39
VALLEY BETWEEN PEAKS 49
WHEN ONE IS ALMOST ENOUGH 55
STEPPING INTO THE VOID 65
SUNSHINE IN THE CITY OF FOG 73
MY OWN PATH FORWARD 81
THE MIRACLE ARRIVES 97
MY ROAD TO YOU 111
    Tears of Hope 112
    Your Beat Is My Addiction 113
    I Want 114
    Patience 115
    The Hardest Things 116
    Two Worlds: Somewhere Between Illusion and Reality ... 118

About Time 120
Things You Cannot Escape From 121
The Dawn of Truth 122
About Options 123
Things to Keep in Mind 124
The Power of Believing 127
They Always Know 128
The Double F Method 129
Trust Your Hidden Power 130
There, But Not 132
In Her Eyes, I Saw Myself 133
He Knows You Can 135
Mind Over Material 136
Final Thoughts 138
Dear Readers 141

*I would dive into the seven seas even
though I do not know how to swim
in order to find you,
my precious abalone.
For you,
I would do it all.
For you,
I dived.*

DEDICATIONS

Above all, to God: You are great, kind, fair and loving. Thank you for everything I have gone through, everything I am going through and everything I will go through. Every day you have given me has taught me something. I may not have understood the lessons then, but I am starting to now. Thank you.

To my husband: My love, my soul mate, papa of my dadas, my beloved companion who has shared with me every feeling I describe in these pages. Words will never be enough to describe the way I feel about you.

To my precious parents: Without your prayers and warmth, I could not have made it this far.

To my readers: For those who have walked the same path as me, we are all in this together, and with God's will and hope, we will have our precious babies. Remember that a fire cannot light without darkness, success does not exist without failure and we cannot stand without falling. We cannot fully grasp the meaning of happiness without first understanding the definition of grief.

To the ones who inspired me to write this book, to the apple of my eye, my true wish, my honest prayer, my future children: Mommy wants you to know that she is brave and would trade anything to feel your sweet and infatuate movements in her belly. Those little kicks that you will make will be the best thing she could ever experience.

INTRODUCTION

It all started with a pure and honest prayer in one of the holiest and most sacred places on earth. The year 2012. Very early one morning, right before sunrise, I put on my head cover and went to pray. The sky was still dark. It was raining heavily, almost like a typhoon. I got soaking wet before I even reached my destination, even though the hotel I was staying in was right across the street. I ran with complete and utter tunnel vision, looking neither left nor right, oblivious to my surroundings. My arms ached as with one hand I pulled my drenched, long black garb that dragged behind me with the weight of water, while adjusting my head cover with the other. I pushed forward, putting one foot in front of the other, determined to reach my destination and never looking back. The squish, squish of my soggy sneakers with every step was the reassurance I needed to know that I was getting closer to my destination. As I felt that I drew closer, my eyes darted in every direction, searching for the green entry signs while watching the flurry of traffic on the road at the same time.

The closer I got, the more crowded and difficult it became. I was with my mother and brother. A few meters separated us. I was always the one running late. When we reached the main entrance, we took off our shoes, placed them in old white plastic covers and gave them to my brother to hold. We held hands tightly, trying not to get separated from one another. We tried for several hours to fuse our thin, exhausted bodies into one of the ring-like queues that were crammed with people. After various attempts and with steely commitment, we managed to find an empty spot large enough for a child. Somehow, miraculously, this tiny space accommodated three adults. We felt beyond lucky to have the spot for five minutes. It sounds like a very short period of time, but it felt like five long, blessed hours of grace. I closed my eyes and made a faithful prayer.

All eyes and bodies faced one direction, giving this unique crowd an identity of its own. It is a scene I cannot begin to describe, a scene like no other. All hands were raised to the sky, eyes upturned, and a myriad of voices cried for the fulfillment of favors and the forgiveness of sins, hearts mumbling thoughts only the Lord heard. Every face told a different story. Every eye held a mystery only the Lord knew. Every life had a secret of its own. The prayers and deeds differed, yet the desire was the same. All hoped their prayers would be answered. I myself prayed for many things, asked for many things, wished for many things. There are some prayers I still remember and some prayers I do not even recall. One of the prayers I made was to become an author. I did not specify how or when or what I would write about. I just prayed to become a writer.

My prayer was heard in a way that still amazes me. God hears all prayers, and accepts all prayers, in His own way. Time allows us to understand some of those ways and others will always remain hidden. Both ways are good, and both ways lead to the same result: the acceptance of the prayer. Forgiveness. Redemption.

But at the time, I had no way of knowing that God heard my prayers and would answer them. Like all of those around me, I had only my blind faith in God that carried me forward.

Suddenly, the rain stopped and God's morning star appeared. A mid-October-like breeze brushed past me, carrying the heavenly scent of amber, and I felt like it was a sign. A silent, invisible command from above willing me to surrender to the serenity of a place that was never empty. Was it a sign?

Does this mean that in this, the holiest of places, all my prayers will be answered? I wondered briefly before surrendering to the moment, letting peacefulness envelop me, obliterating my senses to all of the chaos around me. I had faith, and that was enough.

We finished our prayers, and each of us had three or four cups of cold, refreshing holy water (on an empty stomach) until we were satiated. We walked out. Before leaving, I turned back for one last glance. I had a strange feeling. I whispered one more prayer before the crowd pushed me out.

*****

I have always dreamt of being an author. But I thought that all of the ideas were taken: cooking, love, diet, school, parenting and fashion, you name it. Bookstores were just packed with books. I did not know or even expect that there was something on the horizon that would change my perspective on life, forever. Ideas come from what we face in our lives, and since each one of us has a different life to live and a different destiny to pursue, there will always be something new to write about. As one of my colleagues at work said, "Ideas never end." Our ideas might intersect somewhere, but the way of approaching them will always vary.

One day, right before I began writing this book, I was sitting with one of my friends at work. I asked her, "How do you think writers write books?"

"Writers have quite a relaxed life," she replied with a confident voice and a big smile on her round face. "They get up in the morning, enjoy a warm cup of English breakfast tea and hit the writing pad right after that."

I nodded and muttered to myself, "I wish you were right, my dear friend."

*****

I have always thought that the phrase "two spirits in one body" was just an expression, words put together to form an idiom. Yet when I decided to become a mother, these words triggered a chain of untamed thoughts in my head.

Some people are lucky enough to skim through the chapters of parenthood easily and smoothly. But for my husband and me, this was not the case. This book will share with you what my husband and I have been through and the feelings we have had during the most important journey of our lives. I once read that if you want to feel time, you should write. That is what I am doing today, writing the toughest yet most beautiful moments I have lived.

I do not know about other authors, but for me, great stories come from the deepest pain. Those who have suffered the most look for words to match their feelings and complete the puzzle. Some people experience acute pain, cry a river of tears, lose liters of blood, and plunge to the deepest point of despair to come up with a decent piece of writing. I am one of those people.

In writing this book, some pages made me cry. Some pages made me laugh. Some pages broke me into infinite pieces. Some pages made me hallucinate. Some pages gave me hope. Some pages made me feel alive. And every page was a moment of my life.

Through it all, I have chosen not to reveal my true identity. Many of you will wonder why that would be. The reasons are many, but there is one thing I am certain of: This book does not tell only my story. This is the story of many other couples around the world who have tried and are still trying to conceive, pushing themselves beyond the limits of pain and fear, praying every day to be blessed with the miracle of a new life, a precious abalone. Let us all share this wish, have hope and pray together.

Miracles do not need a specific time to happen, because time is just a notion of the human mind. Miracles descend when a faithful heart whispers an honest prayer to its Creator.

Amen to all our prayers.

I Know What I Want to Be

I have been asked many times what I want to be in life. I remember being asked this question for the first time when I was in kindergarten and I immediately said, "A doctor." I grew up dreaming of becoming a surgeon. I planned to study medicine abroad, and I got accepted to one of the best medical schools in the U.S. But I ended up studying electrical engineering in one of the best schools in town, which is literally 10 minutes away from my parents' house. I felt lucky to stay close to my family and loved ones.

As I continued my studies, I kept wondering and asking myself why I hadn't married when most of my best friends had and when I had received a number of proposals. That all changed one warm summer evening after my junior year in college. I found out that the best sometimes comes last. I was chasing stars when I was destined to have the moon. My neighbor proposed to me and I accepted. It was a memorable proposal followed by the perfect "Yes, I do!" A very special day that I shall never allow myself to forget in its tiniest details.

I met my husband in our living room, right after his family proposed. Yes, ours was an arranged marriage. A lot of people have the wrong perception of arranged marriage. It is not by force. Maybe it used to be, but that was the past and, for the most part and in my case at least, things have changed. The majority of marriages in the Gulf occur in this way.

This is how it usually goes: The family of the bride-to-be sits with her and discusses the matter, listens to her opinion on the subject and asks her if she wants to see the suitable groom that they have already scoped out in an arranged meeting in her house, precisely in the living room. If she agrees to meet with him, his family tells him the time and date, and the meeting takes place. What happened to me was funny. I forgot his face after I left the living room. All I remember was how I babbled on nonstop about how good and talented I was in school. And I remember, too, how when he first walked through the door, I immediately determined him handsome. He was exactly my type, yes. Was I his type? It was just like a blind date, I guess. You sit together and ask questions, getting to know each other. If there is a need to see each other again to get to know each other more, the family of the groom arranges for another date either in the house of the bride-to-be or somewhere public (of course, with a family member joining the not-yet couple). Most of the courtship is spent talking on the phone and meeting in family homes. The bride's family becomes an agency comparable to the FBI, digging deep to uncover all of the important details about the groom that an infatuated potential bride may absent-mindedly forget to consider. How does he make a living? Who are his friends? Does he pray? How often and where? What is his reputation among family, friends, and elders in the community? How does he treat his parents and siblings? What are his manners like? And, most importantly, is he good enough for their precious daughter? Is he truly worthy of her? Is this a good match? The same process can be said for the groom's family when considering their future daughter-in-law.

This process usually takes from two weeks up to two months. When both families agree (and the bride and groom consent to marriage as well), the engagement takes place and a marriage certificate is signed. At this time, the husband gives the wife a certain amount of money as a gift, an unrestricted amount depending on his financial ability. Additionally, as a tradition of our culture that has been observed for decades, it is common for the husband to provide a "dazza", gifts and jewelry to his new wife as a symbol of how families cherish their daughters, and at the same time how the groom respects, values, loves and appreciates their daughter. Most importantly, it shows his commitment to her and how respectful he is of the oath of the marriage contract. I was given a Belgium diamond necklace, bracelet, ring and earrings, a collection of luxury perfumes, and another set of gold jewelry of my own choice.

Our engagement lasted for nine months. My beloved mother took care of wedding preparations from the tiniest details to the biggest decisions. She knew I was busy with school and finals and exams. And being a bride-to-be is hard work too! The added family pressures, social engagements and the commitment to self-care for the big day is, ironically enough, quite stressful as any bride can attest.

I waited for spring semester to finish and made sure I passed all of my courses. The wedding was at the beginning of summer: June 7. I am writing this after seven years of marriage, and I still would say it was one of the most magical and beautiful days of my life (in third place, and I will mention the first and second ranked events later in this book, so bear with me and keep reading). This is the day I called mine. I was truly shining, inside and out. I have never in my life been spoiled like this. Hostesses walked around the room greeting the guests with a waft of luxurious perfumes as they entered the wedding hall at the Ritz Carlton. Floating around on trays to be enjoyed by the hundreds of guests were the finest Swiss chocolates, delectable local pastries, fresh juice cocktails and *hor d'oeuvres* that simply flew off the silverware. Sixty tables were arranged in the grand wedding hall, in the middle of which was a three-foot fine crystal pole with a collection of colorful fresh roses that matched with the silver and gold decorations and crystal tableware for every guest. The maximum capacity of the hall was 500 guests, but more than 600 invitations were distributed. More than 800 guests showed up. It was the event of the season. I was the first daughter and the first grandchild from my mother's side of the family to get married, a fact in itself that made half of the city show up. Thank God I was the bride, otherwise someone else would have taken my seat for sure.

The moment I entered the hall and started walking down the aisle was something beyond what words could ever describe. I wasn't nervous or anxious; I was beaming with the deep satisfaction that this was my day, my moment, and all eyes were on me. I wished it could last forever. The lights were dimmed, candles were lit, and melodies drifted around me. People held their breath in amazement. I breathed with a bit of difficultly as I felt the tightness of my white gown envelop me and gripped my tear-shaped, off-white rose bouquet even tighter. The soft petals entwined between the fingers of my sweaty, ice-cold hands. My mother was standing on my right side, reminding me to smile and not to panic. But she needn't have done that because I was just happy to take it all in. Every step I took down the aisle immersed the guests in a blend of amazement and silence. I felt like an empress making her first appearance before the crowd. My heavily-beaded mermaid gown fit me to perfection and my long white tulle veil floated behind me. My youngest aunt helped in adjusting the gown and dress all the way. She was the only bride's maid. As I reached the wedding arch, she helped me to turn around. The entrance music finished and the DJ was back on. More than 400 guests came to congratulate me. When the time came for my husband to enter the hall, my father and my brothers accompanied him. A special song is played for this moment of the wedding. It is like a greeting and prayer for the groom. The moment I saw him, walking towards me alongside the men I love most, I knew for sure that I had made not only the right choice, but also a wise one.

*****

After the wedding, I faced a new life and a series of wishes and expectations. It's funny how as a girl I dreamed only so far as the perfect wedding; but as a woman, my heart expanded and I knew the meaning of life extended beyond worldly pleasures and I was meant for more: I was meant to be a mother. I wanted with all my heart to get pregnant right after I got married. At this point in my life, the ultimate answer to the question "What do you want to be?" was "A mother."

But a hectic year lay ahead. My senior year in college, tons of exams, homework and long presentations, plus preparing for my senior design project. Who could possibly forget that? I have no idea how I got married at such a busy time. But I have to say, when the right person walks into your life, you will find the time to make room for your destiny. We escaped for a quick, yet amazing, two-week honeymoon, then I got back to real life: a heavy-duty summer course. I had to do it if I wanted to graduate, and my plan to graduate that year would be dashed with even the tiniest of delays.

I never considered motherhood would be one of those delays. For me, it fit in perfectly with the pace my life was going at, at the time. Despite the fact that I had an infinite list of school duties, the desire to become a mama never felt like a burden or something that could wait. I got up every day and wondered if it would be my big day (sorry, I mean our day!). I honestly cannot recall how many times I had my beta blood test done. Every time I took the test and the result was negative, I was devastated. Sometimes I cried my eyes out, and when someone asked what was wrong, I would just reply the same thing over and over again: "Too much school work! It's too much pressure on me!" I couldn't even reveal it to those closest to me. Even though some of them knew, I tried my best to hide it, and the more I hid it, the more pain it caused me.

I graduated a year after my marriage, and realized that I could not use the excuse of "excessive school duties" any more. What would I do next? I tried to come up with new excuses, and tried even harder to convince myself with them. That made my life easier for a while. The list of excuses worked like a cloak. I could hide my body perfectly, but my eyes would never lie.

I realized that I was depriving myself of the most important thing in life: living it. I learned that by focusing on what I did not have, I was losing all of the precious things that God had blessed me with. I decided to change, to be strong, to face the problem and not run away from it. Tears and grief would only get me sympathy, excuses would buy me time (and only temporarily, at that) and that was not what I wanted for myself. I knew I deserved much better, and I could only achieve it if I believed in it. Yes, I believed.

A Difficult Start

Whenever a couple experiences delays in conceiving a child, regardless of the reason, people – from close family members to distant relatives to casual friends – begin suggesting in vitro fertilization (IVF). But many people have the wrong idea about the concept and process of IVF, which is just one possible option in the field of assisted conception. People assume that IVF is the ultimate solution to all conception problems. Well, the first thing anyone who has not been through IVF should know is that nothing is guaranteed, from the first to the very last step. IVF may become the ultimate and 100% guaranteed solution one day, but now it is not.

From an engineer's point of view, I would say the process of IVF is like trial and error. The female body gets prepared by taking stimulating medications for 10 to 14 days, depending on how high a dose the body needs. Age, health and weight are important contributing factors in the duration of treatment. If the body responds well to the treatment, a decent number of follicles of different sizes and quality will be formed.

After that comes the "harvest" stage, when the egg (follicle) collection takes place. At the same time, the male partner must hand in a sperm specimen. Then, in the IVF lab the two specimens (for both male and female) are tested for quality and chromosomal defects. Only the best quality sperm and follicles will be chosen for the process of fertilization. Even then, in some circumstances the fertilization fails. Why? I still do not know. But that is not the trickiest part yet.

Next, fertilization will be cultured in a specific equilibrium in the IVF lab. If the fertilization succeeds, the process of cell division starts and an embryo is miraculously created. After three to five days of cell division, an embryologist examines the quality of embryos that survived the division. The embryos that are of good and surviving quality will be transferred to the uterus. After that, the countdown begins. And the patient is not yet allowed to call herself pregnant. Here is where the survival of the fittest stage starts. Transferring a good grade embryo does not necessarily mean the implantation is guaranteed. Why? Science again fails to provide the answer.

There are many different cases that require IVF or some other type of assisted conception, from blocked fallopian tubes to endometriosis to low sperm count. All of these issues have a reasonable, known explanation in the world of science.

Why did my husband and I require IVF? Until this day, we still don't know. Not yet. Everything occurs due to a certain cause. Humans, in alliance with time and knowledge, may or may not be fortunate in finding a desired and reasonable explanation to the cause. Why is that? With the will of the Lord, today's mysteries are tomorrow's remedies.

Who will be fortunate enough to live and experience that? Imagine if all conception and infertility problems were solved by swallowing a single pill that tasted like cherry, or if we could beat cancer with a vaccine shot similar to those given in childhood. Can that truly be? I think so. One day.

*****

IVF clinics are always extremely overloaded with patients, so the process of getting an appointment was not easy. Lucky for me, I managed to get an appointment that was only a couple of months away. But sometimes things don't go as planned. I received a devastating phone call from the hospital a few days before the date of my appointment. I'll never forget the date of my first appointment, since for me it felt like the true beginning of this entire journey. March 28, 2014: I have memorized it like my own birthdate. So, you can imagine my anticipation for this date to finally come after months of waiting, only to be let down for the first of many times.

I was just finishing a long day at college, and I was on my way home.

"We're sorry for the inconvenience, but your doctor is on leave for a year," a woman's voice, with an accent, said when I answered the call. "Your appointment is shifted to another doctor and you will have to wait for some time."

The phone call ruined all my plans for the week. The news plunged me into shock and frustration because I had planned everything according to that date. All of the excitement that had been building in my ever-hopeful heart washed away leaving it hollow ... for a time.

The void of disappointment quickly filled once again with my everlasting faith. It wasn't meant to be this time, I reassured myself. God had other plans for me. I believe everything happens for a reason – not the doctor's reason, of course – but because of something I did not know. I believe that every delay brings a positive surprise with it. I thanked God for whatever was happening, certain that whatever happened in a strong believer's life was paving the way for good. Besides, this was one of the most important things in my life, and was worth waiting for. It was my beautiful wish, a trusted prayer, and a hope that would never rest or die.

This is something no one tells you about this particular journey to motherhood. You will experience a roller coaster of emotions, the highest of highs and the lowest of lows, sometimes within the span of days or even within the span of seconds. But, of course, you must stay strong, stay the course and always keep moving forward.

I called my husband and spoke with him about the delay, trying hard to hide my disappointment. I tried to contain myself at the beginning, but sometimes in life you cannot pull yourself together to say a simple sentence like, "I'm OK." I knew that for every tear that fell from my eyes, my husband would cry silently thousands on the inside. Though he felt my pain, I tried my best to hold it in tightly.

*****

Love of my life, my beloved husband: To the one who laughs at my jokes, grieves for my pain, loves my cooking and writes the best love notes (don't stop writing them, they bring me pure joy!). God willing, I promise you I will be strong enough to get back up every time I fall, not for my own sake, but for you, for us, for our babies.

*****

We waited. During that time, my husband and I called hundreds of times to check for the availability of earlier appointments, and registered our names on the waiting list. We also spoke to many people in the hospital hoping to get a foot in somehow. We pulled all the strings we knew. After two months of trying, the IVF clinic called. There was one free appointment on the waiting list. We were on cloud nine. That phone call was the best news in such a long time. We were extremely happy and super excited. Finally, God had accepted our prayers. We were officially in.

And those, my dear readers, were the first baby steps of our IVF treatment. But, again, sometimes the wind blows against you. I was seen by a doctor, and given some medication for two weeks, including morning blood tests and ultrasound sessions every other day. Something totally unpredicted happened towards the end of the two weeks. I suffered side effects from the daily injections I was receiving. I got hyper-stimulated. My body started accumulating fluids, mostly in the pelvis and surrounding the kidney, which caused serious abdominal pain. This also meant that I could not retrieve my eggs, because it could be dangerous. My doctor said that it would put my health at risk, because fluids might accumulate on my lungs and that would be enough to cause serious side effects.

The root of the problem was the dose my doctor prescribed me. The dose was inappropriate for my age and weight (I was only 23 and weighed 46kg). My abdominal area was noticeably bloated. I suffered from an acute pain around my kidney. It almost killed me every time I fought for a breath. It turned out that my body had accumulated water around the kidney, putting extra pressure on it and causing the brutal pain, and around the pelvis too. I tried going to the ER to get any kind of pain killer to reduce the pain, but even morphine shots weren't enough. When I called the IVF clinic to talk to my doctor about the side effects, she was not on call and another doctor took the call. I assume this doctor, as well, was used to hearing the sometimes over-dramatic complaints of patients fretting over their condition. She brushed me off and told me that whatever I was feeling was normal. Later, when I saw my doctor at the designated appointment, she said to me, "This happens to 10% of our patients." But later I learned that what I was experiencing was not at all normal: the dose given to me was a dose for someone 30 years old and weighing 60kg. A mistake that could have cost me my life.

All of this forced me to agree to freeze my eggs for a while until my body recovered. The hyper-stimulation I suffered from made it too dangerous to continue the process, because fluids and water could reach my lungs and I could die. There was no way to safely retrieve eggs without risking my life until I recovered. The eggs were frozen until my body returned to normal. Only then could the therapy continue and the frozen eggs be retrieved. It was a setback I hadn't counted on. I was so ready to bring life into this world that I hadn't even considered the very real threat it could pose to my own life.

I stopped getting my period for a while, and experienced hormonal imbalance, mood swings and acute pain in my kidneys. My mood swings were so intense that only a few people, the ones closest to me, could have a simple, short conversation with me. I couldn't bear my own voice. I hated words. I wanted to be alone. I do not know if it was guilt, pain, agony or sadness. I had a kind of aggrieved behavior towards everyone, including myself. Anything could upset me, no matter how small or stupid. I just couldn't handle any sound or voice or face around me. Whatever was going on inside me, it was projecting out fiercely. I was not over-reacting, I was just carrying a heavy burden.

All this made me isolate myself from the people around me, because whenever I saw family or friends they would easily notice that something was wrong and ask a series of infinite questions and demand answers. Honestly, I was running out of excuses and was tired of coming up with lies. So, to avoid that I preferred to be alone until I got back on my feet. This was very hard on me, because it was a very heavy weight to carry. But I knew that I was doing it for something I desired more than breathing air and that was enough to make all the pain tolerable.

*****

In general, as I have learned, frozen embryos have less probability of surviving than fresh ones. Despite that fact, I decided to proceed. It was the only available option at that time. In my situation, even one percent was enough to trigger optimism, a new hope. I got my embryos transferred on October 28, 2014. I had to spend the longest and most challenging two weeks in my entire life awaiting the results.

Not to sound clichéd, but waiting truly is the hardest part. If anything, 90% of the anxiety experienced in the IVF process is from the waiting. Because everything I had worked for, paid for, and prayed for would be revealed after those two weeks. I was bombarded by thoughts, day in, day out ranging from good, bad, to completely crazy. Is it going to work? Is it my time now? That woman is staring at me. Do I look different? Is she giving me the evil eye? I feel good. This is it! What is that pain I feel…? It's never going to happen. All this suffering for nothing! Can I eat that? Will it affect my chances?

It is exhausting to think of one thing constantly for that amount of time. It really hurt my head. The slow ticking sound of the clock annoyed me the most. The silent stare of the calendar gave me the chills. As much as I wanted to spin the wheels of time faster, I had this contradictory feeling when the date of the result drew near. But this is what I wanted to know the most, right? Why am I backing off now? Why now? Am I too weak to face the result? Am I backing off because I lack faith? Or is it just because I am scared? This internal struggle tore me apart, consuming all my energy.

November 11, 2014 was the day my husband and I had been waiting for. We woke up as soon as the sun's light broke over the horizon. We got dressed with particular care and my husband gave me a ride to the hospital. My appointment was at 11:00 am but I showed up at 7:00 am. I was bursting with a blend of excitement and fear, and trying desperately not to stress out and to calm myself down. I checked my emails, watched some vines, made some phone calls, went to the cafeteria. Time refused to pass. The clinic was overflowing that day with women just like me. How many of these women will have their dreams fulfilled today? How many will leave instead with broken hearts?

I went to pray to relieve the stress, and when I got back, the doctor was standing next to the reception desk and calling my name. When I went up to her, she looked right at me and couldn't hold back the news. Her eyes revealed the words before her tongue spilled them. I pushed past her inside the room and lowered myself gingerly into the seat across from her desk.

"Maybe next time," she said shortly.

What just happened? I asked myself in complete confusion and total shock. The only sentence that came out of my mouth before my eyes filled with tears was, "Whatever the result, I shall thank the Lord for it." I wanted to say more, ask questions, and gather some answers, but the words wouldn't come out no matter how hard I tried. I wanted a little bit more control over myself and to hold back my tears, but the weight of the grief on my eyelids made it impossible. A moment later, my cheeks were guttered with a warm and salty river of tears. I sniffled, "Doctor, I would like to register for another round please." With a heavy heart, I left the doctor's room.

I went to the reception to register for another appointment. I had no idea what I said when I was being asked. Every question the receptionist asked, I answered with a heavy nod and sometimes my empty stares would pass for an answer. I attempted to listen, but my hearing failed to keep up with the words. It was a heavy burden for me to handle all by myself at the time. My fingers were shaky. I couldn't sign any paperwork, or even call my husband to come and pick me up.

I chose to stay in the hospital waiting room, alone, for quite some time. I guess I needed to spend some time by myself, without talking, without thinking, and without getting interrupted by anyone or anything. I got lost in my thoughts and memories, and didn't know whether to leave or stay a bit longer because I was not ready to get back to my barren reality just yet.

I walked the grey hallways, visited the outpatient clinics, passed by the lab, and stayed at the newborn clinic for a while. It smelled different. It smelled good.

I did everything to postpone calling my husband to deliver the shocking news. I was not afraid of calling, but every time I dialed his number I hung up before it rang. It was not fear. It was something I could not explain even to myself. Thinking of what I would say suffocated me. I tried many times, but I just could not put up with the elevating pressure on me. Time passed, and faces changed. The rush in the lobby and the hallways dwindled until they were empty and noiseless but for the sound of printers and ringing phones. It was break time and everybody left, including patients and medical staff, except for me. I did not know if my unconscious mind was forcing me to stay or if it was a conscious choice I made.

I was exhausted. I gathered what was left of my energy and finally called my husband. Right before I delivered the bad news, he said, "I know, honey. I am on my way to you." It must have been the shakiness of my "hello." One word, one tone and three seconds summed it up.

People started showing up for their evening appointments. That made it less tense for me, at least. On my way out of the hospital, I saw women getting their beta blood test done and I could guess the result from their happy faces. Some women were carrying sweet little newborns. Other women were lining up in long queues with their round baby bumps registering for appointments. Yet other women were crossing the finishing line and being guided to delivery rooms. I wished I could fuse myself into one of these groups, any of them, as long as it involved a healthy baby.

On our way home, I remained as silent as a pale gypsum statue covered in plastic wrap and placed in a brown paper box in a dark, humid warehouse. I turned my head to the right and attempted to look at the cars and the road. My husband knew I was not merely looking out the window. I managed to hide my face, eyes and tears, but my sobs were too loud to hide. I did not wish to say anything. I just wanted to scream and let the tension, the pain and the pressure out before they broke me. It was too much to handle. It was too much to lift. My mind froze, my body was bleeding, and I was in a state of shock. I stared at the window, contemplating the features of my pale, thin face, trying to match the paths of my tears with the paths the dried rain drops had drawn on the dusty window. I watched each drop cutting its way through from the inside before rolling down my cheeks. My body was present, but my mind strayed far away and lost its way back. The traces my heart drew as a sign for the way back vanished. I wondered if I would make it until tomorrow's sunrise, or go down with today's sunset. It was not a choice of mine to make. It was more of a state of mind that went beyond my control. I did not lose myself, but I struggled to recognize myself. I never asked myself who I was, and I never will. At that time my only question was what had I become?

The first attempt was a dark time, I admit that. But although it made me grieve for months, it taught me something I wish I had known before. Whenever you feel like letting go, don't, because you are getting closer to what you want. Hope fiercely when your case seems hopeless. Pray strongly when the options fade one after the other. As long as you have made it to today, there is new hope for tomorrow.

*****

It must be said that my first doctor made the initial trial hard for me which I believe had a major impact on how I responded to the treatment. On a marvelous wall at Vejthani Hospital in Thailand, there is a quote that reads: "I don't want you to be only a doctor, but I also want you to be a man." Humanity matters as much as medicine and physical treatment. I do not like to judge people immediately; maybe they have had a rough day, received bad news, or some other unseen negative issue bothers them. Whatever it is, you can never truly tell what a person has experienced that day or over a lifetime so it is best to meet someone with an open heart and mind. When it came to my doctor, I tried to come up with all possible excuses until I ran out of them completely and got fed up entirely.

Dear Doctor,

If my faith has taught me anything, it is to rise above. I felt dismissed, misguided and lost under your care. The Hippocratic Oath that you have sworn states, "First do no harm." Harm can be both physical and emotional. And while my body suffered no permanent harm under your care, your indifference shattered my soul and psyche. Your attitude made me reject everything, including the therapy itself.

In that time and space when I wanted nothing more than to be a mother, I was angry that things with you were so difficult. Aside from the worry and general stress of the IVF process, I was going through it all with someone who I felt lacked empathy.

But, dear Doctor, hindsight is a wonderful thing. I could look back at you in anger and blame you for what happened but I choose to look back at the lessons you forced me to learn. God put me in a difficult situation, crossing my path with yours during an already emotional time in my life, to teach me that I can push through adversity, no matter how difficult and come out stronger for it. With you, I learned that I need to advocate for myself. I learned that I need to be patient. And most importantly, I learned that I need to forgive. I am acknowledging you here because though I will not forget our tumultuous relationship as patient and caregiver, I will not (and did not!) let you stand in the way of my dream. I let go of any hurt, pain or anger you caused because, to quote a wise man, "I have no desire to suffer twice, in reality and then in retrospect."

Signed,
A Warrior

With this letter, forever in the pages of this book about my trials and triumphs, I close the pages of a difficult chapter in my life.

Drawing Strength from Others

Days passed quickly, and our second cycle approached. This time I was very positive about it. I read uplifting quotes and books and took some days off work to focus on myself and to rest physically and mentally. I watched amazing videos about the miracle of pregnancy and birth and imagined myself in those videos. I did all I could to stay optimistic. I needed to push myself a little bit forward and not let the first trial affect me as much as it had initially. I could see the light at the end of the tunnel this time. My husband and I started picking names for our baby and paint colors for the nursery. I was practicing self-actualization: if I considered myself pregnant and truly believed it, I hoped my body would be welcoming to the precious gift I so badly wanted.

During the second attempt, both physically and mentally, I responded better to the treatment, which was really helpful in keeping me upbeat. Upon my request, I was lucky enough to have been transferred to another doctor, one who I immediately took a liking to and from whom I felt a positive energy and strength that I could draw upon. I considered it a new beginning. On this road, I have met many nurses, lab technicians and doctors, but I have to say that this doctor was amazing and unique. Although the treatment phase was the same, she made it feel easier. I was truly blessed to have found not only a doctor, but also a mother, sister and friend. I found a doctor who listened before she spoke, understood before she judged, and behaved like a true mother rather than a stranger in a white coat. Every person on earth from the beginning of humanity has a certain trait that makes him/her like no other. Hers was not giving up on the people who needed her. IVF treatments involve many difficult procedures that require money, time and effort. In a hardship like this, a person needs a lot of encouragement, faith, confidence and all possible strength. In my case, I thank God infinite times for having a truly supportive husband, great parents and the amazing Dr. Thoraya. In Arabic, "thoraya" refers to the fine luminous lamps that are used to light up mansions and palaces. Her name said everything about her unique personality. She was luminous, inside and out. It was all the little things she did for us that made a huge difference: her smiles, kind words and positive attitude. One person can make an enormous difference.

Besides my doctor, I met many other wonderful people in the IVF clinic. I heard a lot about their inspiring stories, and the difficulties and losses they had been through. I shared mine with them too. Even when there was a large age gap between us, we laughed, cried and wondered together, and became friends. We shared our dreams, named our future kids, and picked their schools and study programs. This was not wishful thinking. This was how much we were certain we would have babies in the future.

It was 12:15 am in the delivery ER, and I was preparing for the second round. I showed up for an injection at that specific time as a final preparation for the egg retrieval procedure a day later. I registered my name, received a number and waited for a while with my eyes watching carefully the noisy, ticking, silver clock. It was so strange to be surrounded by a group of women with watermelon-sized baby bumps and be the only one with a flat stomach. I wondered what it would be like when I became like them. I yearned to be a part of that group.

A sharp voice broke the silence of the reception area. The head nurse was calling my number. I walked hurriedly after her, following her fast steps as we entered the delivery unit. She asked me to wait until one of the rooms became available and a nurse could assist me. A moment after that, I saw a group of nurses approaching, and immediately rushed towards them and showed them the injection paper. There was an Indian nurse standing to the side and facing me. I did not notice her presence at first, but she took the paper and guided me to one of the empty rooms. I lay down on the sterile cold white bed and waited for her to finish some paperwork outside. She came in shortly, faced the steel counter and prepared the injection.

"Is it your first time, dear?" she asked.

With a lump in my throat, I said, "Nope. This is my second round."

She smiled and turned around to face me, and said with a soft and comforting voice, "I am an IVF patient myself. I have done it five times so far and none of them were successful."

There will always be people who have worse and tougher conditions than you. Take a minute and think of them. Pray for others and be certain that God will accept your prayers. Was meeting that nurse a coincidence? I do not know, but I am certain that her pep talk helped me to hang in there and pray more, to pray for others and not just myself.

I remember telling my doctor that I couldn't handle two consecutive failed cycles. She sighed and said with a smile on her face, "You are talking about two attempts here? I remember a patient who tried more than 30 times and then got pregnant with beautiful twins. She came here recently for another try!" I never met that woman, but I was stunned by what I was told. I salute her! How strong could she be to bear that tremendous amount of loss? After my doctor told me that story, I realized that I couldn't win if I didn't lose. The most invaluable things in life are earned. The definition of earn here is that you buckle down, risk it all and take your chances.

My mother once said, "Never compare yourself or your life to others. If you do that, you will end up living their lives and trust me, my daughter, you do not want to do that. Every life story has a different plot. Make yours unique. Make it worth living." As always, she was absolutely right. After my first IVF attempt failed, I started comparing my condition to other patients' conditions. It made me float motionlessly in an ocean of stress, trying desperately to look for answers that had no questions in the first place, lost, terrified, and not knowing what my mysterious destiny had in store for me in the next round.

*****

To the most amazing mother in the world: No words will ever suffice to describe everything you have done for me. With your presence, grace descends, your prayers open the doors of heaven, and your concerned phone calls make my day even better. Though sometimes you forget the exact date of my birth, you never allow yourself to forget a second of the day I was born. I thank the Lord thousands of times every day for granting me a mother like you: caring, loving, supportive and so passionate. You are a true gift. You are a blessing. From you, I learned about love before first sight and experienced the strongest connection in life. In your womb, every moment was a life-time wonder. You carried me with love that taught me how to forgive. You carried me with strength that taught me how to fight. You carried me with patience that taught me how to survive reality.

I remember once I felt so lonely and needed you so badly, but we were far away from each other, in two different countries. I told you that if I could go back and stay in your womb, I would not hesitate for second.

I meant it. I needed it so much. Mother, you are a wonder.

All of your advice turned out to be a key that unlocked another door in my life. Thank you for your priceless keys and thank you for being my mother.

*****

During the two-week wait between embryo transfer and implantation in my second IVF round, something I was not ready for at all happened. I started bleeding. I convinced myself that it was spotting from the embryo's implantation. But as time passed the bleeding got heavier and I couldn't wait another day (I was supposed to do the beta blood test in a couple of days). I went to see my doctor the next morning. I waited in the clinic without a scheduled appointment. They refused to let me in, and I refused to leave. I insisted on waiting in the hallway.

I stood for a long time, so long that my feet burned and my back ached. I crossed my arms against my chest and leaned on a wall that had just been painted white. I could smell the strong, sharp scent of fresh paint. The leaning helped reduce the pain a little. I shifted my weight from one leg to the other in a hopeless dance to ease the pain but it was inevitable that soon my feet burned and throbbed. I almost felt like I myself was implanted in that old, grey vinyl flooring, after hours of standing in the same spot, just gazing at the clock and contemplating the hour and minute hands as they ticked by, losing myself in the nonstop noise and hectic movement all around me. The clinic was extremely busy that day and all seats were occupied for hours on end.

When I spotted my doctor coming in, I snuck towards her office.

"Your appointment isn't today, is it?" she said with surprise.

I explained to her what had happened, and she immediately ordered a blood test and registered a clinic appointment in the system. I rushed to the lab and had the blood test done. Her immediate concern sparked my own anxiety, and though I tried all possible techniques to relieve my spiral into despair, nothing worked. I was so tense that I couldn't reply to the simplest questions the lab technician asked. She had to ask me everything at least three or four times and gently poked me to get my attention.

I waited impatiently in the clinic reception area, and finally, after hours of waiting for a place to sit and rest, I found an old plastic chair close to my doctor's examining room. The back of the stiff, unpadded chair was very cold. It made my stomach hurt more than it already did from the tension. I kept shifting my body weight right and left in the unsteady chair with wobbly legs, attempting to distract myself before my number showed in red on the black LED screen.

The result was supposed to come out after one hour, but there were too many patients having their blood test done so it took nearly three hours. The doctor called my name. She looked at the computer, and then looked at me and said, "Don't stress yourself out, dear. It will happen sometime. Look on the bright side, you still have frozen embryos. Don't forget that!"

The shock was not as sharp as the first time around. The bleeding sort of paved the way for me, so I was ready to hear the news. But I still was not ready to believe it in that very moment. This type of psychological conflict drained a lot of my mental and physical energy. It was like a fatal attraction that heaved me into a web that my own hands had unconsciously woven, and I was not doing anything to stop it.

There was one thread of hope that I clung to: my frozen embryos. I do not deny the fact that the feeling of defeat controlled all my emotions and behavior, but I didn't bend to devastation and I never will. A bright side always exists. A new hope and a new attempt. I immediately decided to go for another round. I didn't give my body any time to rest and recover.

Throughout this ordeal, some people would tell me to be strong and have hope. But why did I need any of that when I had faith? It simply included all of the above. This round had also taught me something important. The bigger the wish, the deeper and harder the prayers must be. When we pray, God certainly listens and that is why He pushes us to pray in the first place. Learning from yesterday to survive today is a blessing. Not knowing what will happen tomorrow is also a mercy, because it gives us hope. Having faith is enough to take you through all of that and bring you back to safety. The more you believe in your prayers, the greater the chance they will be answered.

Leave it to faith. Pure and honest prayers are a different kind of magic. They can fix the broken, heal the wounded, fulfill wishes, and make those beautiful dreams that you never wish to wake up from into reality, and, guess what, better than you ever expected.

This round taught me not to give up on what I truly wanted, even when all the signs showed the exact opposite. I met many people in this round, including patients and doctors. A number of those people disappointed me in many ways. That was a huge problem for me. So, whenever I used to have negative thoughts or hear something that could drag me down, I would remember the happy memories and start living them again because happy memories can save us. I reminded myself how strong I was for making it this far, how mysterious tomorrow is, and how much hope it will bring when its sun rises. People will always make predictions and guess conclusions, and it is up to you if you want to confirm them. In many life situations, things get narrowed down to one of two options. You can let other people guess and forecast ideas on your behalf. This will make your life easier in the short-term because you do not have to bother making your own choices, though you may pay a greater price later. Or, you can let your faith, prayers and strong belief in what you think is right draw the map of your own destiny. The choice is yours to make.

*****

I did not know what the number of my winning round would be, but I was certain that I would need not one or two rounds of IVF for it to take, but many. Sometimes I wondered what would happen if I did not need IVF. But in a strange way, I look back on it as a blessing because it showed me the true characters of the great people God has placed in my life – my loving husband, wonderful parents, and an amazing doctor and IVF friends. Without this struggle, I may have never understood the depths of their loyalty, love and compassion. Throughout all this, these people helped push me forward, and with God's will above all, it would hopefully be.

I entrusted my wishes to the Creator, so that He could make wonders out of them. Every detail in our destiny has a purpose, from the little issues we tackle every day to the biggest dilemmas we face. From the people we meet to the things we fall in love with. It is all set for a cause. We might explain away a lot of what we experience as coincidence because we lack the cause. But from what I see, if something happens, then it is surely meant to be. In other words, I call them incidents and not coincidences.

Everything happens for a reason. With patience and faith, you can fit the pieces of the puzzle together and understand the cause when the right time comes. Never rush it, because God will make it up there when you believe in it down here. Pray and believe in it in order to achieve it.

Valley Between Peaks

The day of my frozen embryo transfer had finally arrived. I was so excited and fully focused and prepared both mentally and physically to meet my future baby. I woke up with the first light, prayed and got dressed. I didn't really have an appetite to eat anything at all. I was constantly staring at my wrist watch, holding my phone close, in case I got an early phone call, although I knew the lab did not call before 8:00 am. I hardly swallowed sips of warm water and waited for them to sooth my dry throat. Considering the mental state I was in, my husband suggested driving me to the hospital, and I very much welcomed the suggestion. The closer we got, the faster my heart accelerated. I looked at the trees, the cars and the people to distract myself from whatever was left of my attention. It would have been much easier if it was all just a nightmare. I would eventually wake up and it would all be over. But it was a reality that I could not break free from. I was the first to arrive at the clinic. Only a few doors separated us from my lovely babies. I called the IVF lab to confirm my appointment. A nurse answered and asked me to call again 30 minutes later, because the results were not ready yet. I waited with bated breath for the minutes to pass. I called again after exactly half an hour. My heart was racing so fast that I could hear my heartbeat in my ears. My fingers were ice cold and shaking, and I broke into a cold sweat when it started ringing. Another nurse answered and asked for my name and medical number. I could barely hear her typing my information into the computer over the drum of my nervous heart.

"Sorry, dear, your embryos did not make it," she said in that unmistakable tone.

The words were like a furious storm that slapped me in the face, forcing me into a deep and ruthless silence, and drowning me in a helpless state. I did not resist it. Words that struck me like a series of unsparing waves hitting an abandoned lighthouse in the immense darkness of the night. A single tear slid down my bloodless cheeks, and a moment later many more followed. If physical pain hurts, emotional pain destroys us. I was unable to speak. All the words accumulated in my throat and made it difficult for me to breathe. It burned. My tongue was paralyzed. I barely took a breath and hung up.

I was sitting in the waiting area. Many patients were there. Shimmery tears found their direct path to my chin from my blurred eyes. I tried to close my eyes to stop them from watering more than they already were. I tried to blink away my tears. I did all I could in my power to keep the crying quiet and inconspicuous.

I changed my posture to face any wall to hide my face, but I was sitting right in the middle row. Waves of shock rippled through my body from my head to my toes, conquering my being from its very core to the tips of every nerve, shutting down my whole body. I was unable to walk. My body shutdown. It took me a few minutes to get back to myself. To get back to sanity. To connect to the world around me. To process what had happened to me and return myself to the present. I forced my way through the crowded row of patients, hemmed in by a sort of unseen concrete barrier. It stopped me from progressing. Was I the only one feeling this? Could anybody around notice that too?

I drew a number and requested to see my doctor. When my number came on, I could barely pull myself together to walk towards her room. It felt like I was swimming through mud, and the closer I got, the thicker and deeper it became. The rusty chains of numbness and fear were attached to my limbs, and the heaviness on my chest dragged me to the deepest point of despair. Whatever she asked I replied to tonelessly, and just shook my head in response. My stifled sobs made it difficult for me to speak properly.

I knew that at some point it would get better, much better, and instead of a ray of light I would see the whole sun. But it was so difficult to convince myself of that back then.

My doctor advised me to take another appointment as soon as possible, because it was nearly summer. It got very busy at that time of year, literally like summer clearance sales at Harvey Nichols. I rushed to reception and registered for the next available trial. It was four months away.

After dragging myself through a long and difficult day at the hospital, I went to my safest place: home. I put on anything I found in my closet. I snuck under my heavy pink woolen blanket. I spent some time alone. No sounds or movement. No thoughts or actions. Just alone, in isolation.

When I was ready, I texted my husband and then deleted the message right after it was delivered. I did not want to keep reading it. It made it harder every time I read the text to myself. I did not realize that I was crying until the phone screen was covered in tears. The screen stopped responding to my fingers' touch and I had to wipe off my bitter tears with my light cotton pajama shirt. The phone automatically shut down. If small drops of tears had the power to shut down a device, what would they possibly do to a vulnerable body? What would they do to a bleeding heart? What would they do to me? Would I shut down forever?

I screamed, quite loudly. Not to create a scene or demand sympathy, but to release the flaming embers that were burning me up inside. I fought off a dangerous feeling to free myself from the deadly choking grip that was almost killing me.

I remembered I hadn't eaten anything since the night before, hadn't slept well and hadn't spoken to anyone besides the medical staff. I fixed myself some food to fuel me with the energy my body needed to keep standing. I ate without tasting. I slept without resting. I spoke aloud, to the empty house that would never reply back, without feeling or even realizing what was coming out of my mouth. I knew they were words, but I had no idea what I mumbled. When the heart cries, it hurts more than the eyes. It cries pure bitterness.

Perhaps I should have given myself more time between the second and third attempts. Did I ask too much of myself? I always thought of how fast time goes by, but not when the right moment comes. The race against time was harder than I expected it to be.

My husband came home. He calmly approached me. We did not speak to each other. He snuck under my blanket and gave me a warm look that said thousands of words. He took my thin, cold, lifeless body in his warm arms and hugged me close to his heart and rubbed my back, like a child. I rested, in peace.

*****

My strong desire to become a mother made me forget about all the pain I had just encountered. I realized that giving up was giving up on my life, and I was just not ready for that. It did not matter how hard it got, because that was nothing compared to what I wanted and dreamt of having.

Maintain the spark of hope, and shield it with faith. It is the fuel of your desire.

The curve of life keeps on surging and each coordinate contributes to increasing the degree of difficulty of this curve, thus making it hard to analyze. When you reach the peak of it, ask yourself, "Could it get any worse?" If you think about it for a second, no peak remains constant. It will stabilize in one condition, if and only if you gave it all up there. Always look on the bright side. To enjoy a magnificent view, you have to reach the mountain top. Yes, the adventure is risky, but it makes you do great things, and as they say, what doesn't kill you makes you stronger. The curve never stays as it is. It either curves up or down, and becomes a memorable story printed on a page of the history of the universe, marked: A page to remember, under the luminous galaxies. On a mountain crest, once upon a time, hope was born.

I believe it when people say that life is a roller coaster. I used to think it was just a metaphor. We are forced to ride it and receive our ticket the day we are born. Sometimes it slows down and sometimes it goes faster than the blink of an eye. Our reaction towards the ups and downs of life determines the coordinates that form the behavior of the curve.

Maintain true faith in God and a strong belief in your prayers, draw hope and love from the people around you, and strength from believing deeply in yourself and what you do. I made a prayer and believed in it. I made a wish and worked hard for it. I made a promise to myself and I kept it. Pray often, dream big, and believe as if your prayers and dreams were already a reality.

When One is Almost Enough

Even though a decent number of eggs was retrieved this round, only one made it to the blastocyst stage, which is when the embryo reaches Day 5 of cell division. When the embryo reaches this stage, the chances of pregnancy increase and a transfer can be made. We decided to go ahead with the single embryo. I did not know if I was making the right decision at the time, but I knew that any sacrificing mother would do the exact same thing: chase success against all odds, hoping and believing that it will unite her with the child she has been waiting for.

My husband and I went against an important recommendation made by our supervising doctors. We knew that it was a huge risk, but we couldn't afford to lose this chance. I guess we were not ready to give up yet. We were told that our embryo should be frozen, otherwise there would be a great chance that it wouldn't survive until all the tests were done. Something within me told me to refuse the freezing idea, and I immediately did. We were warned that it would be under our complete responsibility if the embryo failed to progress. We could have agreed to it, but every parent knows what suits their child best, and we knew freezing would diminish the only chance left this time. It was not just a feeling we had, it was parental instinct.

I waited for five days after the egg retrieval procedure. After that, I received a phone call from the lab informing me to prepare myself for the embryo transfer. When I arrived, I was asked to drink at least one liter of water and not use the toilet (embryo transfer is done best on a full bladder). My vital signs were taken and later I was given a long white gown, a thin hair net and sterilized blue shoe covers. After I got dressed and settled, an embryologist was waiting for me in the operating room. She gave me a pink paper that had all my information on it and asked me to sign it. She pointed right at the middle of the paper and said, "You have got only one average blastocyst left for transfer."

I first thought one was such a small number. Was it enough? I asked myself. I strongly believed this remaining embryo had survived that far for a reason. It was a sign for me to carry on. It was a sign that we made the right decision. The doctor proceeded and explained to me that my embryo was not a Grade A embryo, meaning that the probability of hatching was low. Low, yet still possible, I convinced myself. I also remember her telling me that she was discussing my case with embryologists in the lab earlier that morning about not transferring an embryo with a Grade B or C. I insisted on my decision. I wanted my baby back inside my body. Science alone would not, could not, trump my faith.

The right choice is not a sentence written in a book in order to be followed or a statement said to you by others to persuade you. It is a state of mind that only a confident believer can maintain.

I had it back, although I had been warned by my own doctor and the embryologist several times that it might not implant. I am not leaving you behind, my child. Our unity is our strength, I said to myself as I watched the screen while the transfer was being held. A small dot, a bubble, appeared to be swimming inside my uterus. Like a little bird that had been set free. My child, you belong with me. I was given a copy of my baby's ultrasound picture and I kept it under my pillow. I looked at it every day and prayed. Sometimes, I would hold it and talk to it for long hours.

*****

October 4, 2015: a day that I shall never forget. The day I was told that I was going to become a mother. It had happened: the embryo implant had been successful, and we had done it at last! God always listens. God always hears our prayers.

I looked high and low for synonyms for how I felt during this chapter of my life. I Googled many happiness quotes and thought that they might come in handy, and read pieces of creative writing too. The truth is, out of the thousands of words and hundreds of phrases, I was not able to find a single line that described this breath-taking miracle, not even something close to what I was feeling. Every person on the face of this earth is a miracle. And now, this miracle baby was growing inside of me, a miracle myself. It was finally my turn. The strength, faith and love of one miracle carrying another.

On that beautiful day, my tears of happiness and joy rang the bells in the hearts of those who had forgotten what hope means and what strong faith bequeaths in our lives. While it is a fact that happiness and hope are feelings, on that day, believe it or not, I had the chance to dance with them. It was a magical moment, sprinkled with a little bit of star dust. People draw and paint portraits and take pictures that are worth thousands of words, and I lived a moment that left me literally speechless in every sense of the word.

I did not know what tomorrow's tides would bring me, but those gorgeous and incredible seconds that declared the beginning of a new life created within me were and will always be the most cherished and precious time in the entire book of my life. Whether it takes some time or happens immediately, and whether it is planned or unexpected, every pregnancy is a blessing from the Creator and every birth story is indeed a miracle, raw and unfiltered.

*****

I have always wondered what makes a person so special, accepted and loved by everyone. How do some people have deep impact on other people's lives by doing the simplest things? Is it money, compliments, gifts, extra care, sacrifices, or perhaps just a smile? Every situation calls for certain reactions, indeed. In my case, it was something entirely different. In fact, I was lucky and blessed to be put in the gentle hands of a great woman who I will never allow myself to forget. The woman who I was proud to call my doctor: the beautiful (inside and out) and brave Dr. Thoraya.

She was the real behind-the-scenes hero who made many things in this arduous journey less complicated and intense and certainly more beautiful. She offered me three of the most precious gifts I could ask for. She gave me all the time I needed to express my feelings, clarify my doubts, and ask all the questions in the world without rushing me. She smiled always and that itself is enough to calm any patient down. She gave me all the emotional support I needed, treating me as a family member and not merely as a patient. I believe this is enough to make any patient lucky to have her as a doctor. Many people can become doctors, good ones even, but very few deserve to be called heroes. It is never about the amount of knowledge or scientific information attained from books or research, it is simply about humanity.

*****

Dr. Thoraya, when you read this, know that you give the word "hero" its true meaning. You have earned it, because you deserved it.

*****

I might forget names, but I never forget faces, especially of those beautiful nurses who supported me until the beta test result came out. Jane, Mercy, Evelyn, Amal and many more were always there, not only for me but for all the patients. They were excited and grateful just like I was when I heard the happiest news of my life. I witnessed the joy and prayers in their eyes every time I passed by even after I became pregnant. They were empathetic, selfless and caring. This definitely made them no less than heroes too. They showed me the true meaning of sisterhood.

*****

October 4, 2015, brought me a happiness that words could never explain. November 15, 2015, blindsided me with a shock that I did not see coming.

On a warm and calm night, after leaving my parent's house, I started feeling some cramps. Painful, yet tolerable. When I got home, the pain started increasing significantly. It pervaded me, like a drop of ink that spreads through the finest features of a fingerprint. Slowly, then fast, until it covers the whole print. Nothing I tried made it at least stop for a few seconds so I could catch a decent breath. The cramps came every 15 minutes. Then every two minutes. My skin had turned a shade of yellow, then gradually grey, then pale enough to look lifeless. I curled up, hugging my knees to my chest tightly in the hope of relieving a fraction of what I was experiencing. It barely sufficed. For a couple of seconds, maybe. I do not remember. My insides were in a complete state of mayhem. My eyes stared at the ceiling whenever the ache gave me a chance to fight for a breath. Then the pain hit again, and it felt like I was taking a step back from the present, from life itself. When the pain reached its peak, I felt the urge to push. My husband held me close and carefully. I leaned my thin body against his warm chest, wrapping my weak arms around his waist, and holding the back of his shirt.

He slowly helped me walk towards the toilet. With stumbling steps, we barely reached it. The need to push came again and I tried to resist it. A strong feeling inside me prevented me from pushing.

Please do not leave my body. I promise I will take good care of you. I ask you to give me another chance. I beg of you, my child.

I grabbed hold of the edge of the ice-cold white porcelain sink using whatever strength my legs could provide to support my life-drained body. I spread my legs a little and noticed drops of blood starting to spot the bathroom floor. A few moments later, the bleeding increased as blood poured out in slow motion, staining my thighs, reaching my feet, and covering the spot I was standing on. I placed my right hand between my thighs to make sure you wouldn't fall to the ground. Another push, the last, and we were detached. Two warm pieces of flesh the size of a ripe peach, one slightly smaller than the other, rested in the palm of my hands. I had no idea which sac contained you. I was afraid to touch them. I was afraid I might accidentally hurt you.

I imagined you alive in there, waiting to be rescued, wanting to breathe for the first time. Blood dripped from my right hand. I brought you close to my heart, letting you listen to my heartbeat one last time before I let you go. Crimson stained my entire body, the sink, the floor. Everywhere I looked. The bathroom looked like a butcher's shop.

I had waited to hold you for so long, but not like this. This was not what I had imagined. This was not what

I had prepared myself for. This was not what I expected. The moment I held you was the exact moment I lost you. Forever. The connection was gone, and it took away a piece of me with it. You were gone, and I collapsed. With you, I miscarried my heart.

*****

June 8, 2016, was supposed to be my due date. It could have been my baby's birthdate. I will never allow myself to forget that. Who could possibly forget the birthdate of their first baby? I hoped by that time that a beautiful wish would become a reality.

It was not the physical pain that concerned me. It was the emotional dagger that stabbed my heart deeper and stronger every time I remembered that I lost my little one. My precious baby was resting in peace. That is what I was told: the heartbeat and growth stopped at the eighth week. I still believed it was there, beating like it never did before. I never gave up on it, so that it would hopefully never give up on me. I believed in miracles, and I would hopefully witness one soon.

Even though the pregnancy ended at an early stage, sharing my womb, food, drinks, thoughts and blood with that little one created a different and special kind of bond, love and affection. I did not know exactly how to classify it. It was the strongest connection my heart, body and soul had ever felt. This was love before first sight. This was motherhood. I was not objecting to God's will, I was simply grieving the loss of a loved one. Thank you, God, for the best eight weeks I ever lived. I truly wished, strongly prayed and deeply hoped that the next miracle would stay until the end and make its way to my arms, alive, healthy and smiling.

I thought my book would end when this attempt succeeded. I had no clue that another unexpected event would change the entire route of this chapter.

I asked myself: Do I have any idea of what I am doing? What am I up against? What am I truly afraid of losing? The answer was: me, myself and I. I was afraid of losing myself at some point down the road. Losing a baby that I had always wanted was extremely painful for me, but losing myself for a long time after that was a million times harder and more painful. I worried a lot, feared food and motion, doubted the unknown. That drowned us both in an ocean of uncertainties. Forgive me for that, my love. I forgot that if God wants it to be, it will be.

*****

My beautiful baby: I bought you your first pajamas and hung them in my closet. I chose a sweet name for you. Don't take so long to come to us because Mommy and Daddy are waiting for you. We vow to be strong for you. We vow to fight to the last breath in our bodies to have you sleeping in our arms. We vow to do everything we can to unite with you again. It is painful, and we know that. It is fragile, and we know that. Despite all that, we want you and you know that.

Stepping into the Void

Just when I thought things would follow a plan, destiny surprised me in another way. On March 21, 2016, two options were placed on the table. One: jumping off a cliff. With or without a parachute? Destiny and time would tell. Two: putting my bare hands in a lion's den. Abandoned or occupied? Destiny and time would tell.

I had to choose between two difficult options, not knowing the consequences of either. One was to retrieve the embryos if they survived to Day 5 (became blastocysts) without freezing them or screening them (to check for any genetic abnormalities). The second was to undergo pre-implantation genetic screening (PGS). That meant that if the embryos survived to Day 5, they would be sent to a different lab in a different country to check for genetic abnormalities. I did not know how long this process took, but was told that the embryos must be kept frozen, and, hopefully, be retrieved after one month if they survived the journey. No one ever said life was going to be easy.

The clock never stops ticking, and after much deep and honest prayer, a choice was made: take the second option. May my prayers get accepted and may my good deeds be my redemption.

*****

My dear babies: Your father and I fought pain, doubts and tears to have you in our arms. Be strong this time, be strong for us and for the sake of the family we wanted the most from the first day we met. Please. Your father and I do not have any idea of how this chapter will finally end, and we cannot even picture it in our heads right now. But we are certain that the best is yet to come. Life is about anticipation, great anticipation indeed.

*****

I found a wonderful quote written by an anonymous author under a picture of a lovely sleeping newborn baby on an inspiring Instagram account. It said: "This is what always has been the essence of life: disappointment comes before hope, hurt comes before love, and dark comes before brightness to make us realize how important their presence is."

Finally, the results of the PGS were back. I received a call from my doctor informing me that only one embryo was completely normal and was ready to be transferred. My husband and I booked an appointment and had the transfer done, and things went perfectly well. Days went by so fast.

The day before the beta blood test, my sister-in-law threw a high school graduation party for her youngest daughter, Sarah. My husband told me it was fine if

I decided not to go. He knew that I stressed out a lot during the two-week waiting period, especially when it got towards the grand finale. I usually avoided parties, crowded places, or shopping for any reason (I left that chore to my husband during the IVF cycle). I preferred to rest at home most of the time, lay down, eat healthy food, stay away from people, and take a couple of days off duty. Despite the fact that I was freaking out because the test was only a few hours away, I made up my mind to go.

"I am going tonight, honey. I need to shake off the stress a little," I said to him while I was taking a warm shower, dancing slowly and singing to my little one. I hoped he heard me. I had this strange feeling it was a baby boy. I bought Sarah a bracelet from Tiffany and wrapped it nicely. I remember not putting on too much make-up because I did not want my body to absorb a lot of chemicals from beauty products. I filled in my eyebrows softly and put a touch of pink blush on my cheeks and chin. I wore a pink and orange silk cocktail dress with a white orchid print by D&G. The soft Japanese sleeves caressed my skin as I slipped it on over my shoulders. It was flowy and feminine and the embodiment of a midsummer day. I had a pair of heels that matched perfectly with it, but I didn't want to take any chances. I opted instead for a comfortable pair of soft golden leather flats that I had just purchased from Zara. I opened the shoe box and unwrapped the sandals from the vibrant tissue paper and inhaled that incomparable scent of brand-new shoes – nothing smells better – just as the crystal embellishments caught the light and sparkled. Adding simple floral earrings from Chanel as my only accessory, I was dressed. I tried to style my hair in French braids without using a blow dryer because I thought it would elevate my body temperature. Yes, maybe that was just a little bit too much. Well, a lot too much, I know! But I could not help it. I think many mothers-to-be would do the same or even more if they were in the same situation.

When I finished, I stood before a mirror and looked at myself. I looked like a child off to a birthday party: innocent, giddy with optimism, and just plain happy. As I stared at the reflection before me, I prayed that the feeling would last.

*****

When the time came for us to do the beta test to confirm whether the embryo had implanted, the country was on a holiday break and all the private labs were closed. To be honest, that made it a little less tense for me because the more I could delay the test date, the more relief for me. I could not really push back the date more than three days, so on July 9, 2016, I did the test after my grocery shopping. We waited for an hour or so, but I did not call this time. I just could not do it. I was too excited and terrified at the same time. So my husband and I went to the lab to pick up the result. I stayed in the car and he went in. I kept thinking of what to say to him when he came back. Did I say, "We did this, my love," or "Congrats, Baba," or "Let's go to a baby shop right now," or "Say cheese!"? I even practiced some silly dance moves and laughs and prepared my phone video camera to film this amazing life moment that we had waited so long for. I had counted the days and hours to do this, and was more than ready. My hands were shaking, and I started breathing irregularly and sweating even though the air conditioning was turned on to the max. It was intense. I could not hold the phone properly to video the happy moment.

Five minutes later, my husband came out, without any expression on his face. He's tricking me this time, I said to myself. He opened the car door, got in quietly, fastened his seatbelt, and peered at the white envelope with the results. He did not make eye contact with me or say a single word. I continued to look at him, narrowed my eyes, wrinkled my face, and almost reached over to the driver seat to poke and tickle him to get him to look at me and break the happy news. He heaved a deep, long sigh and continued not to look at me. I remember that quiet very well. He placed his right hand on my left shoulder and softly said, "Thank God for everything we have been through. It did not happen yet, my love. There is no pregnancy."

I knew he was not joking, but I seriously did not understand the words he had just spoken. I gazed into his eyes. It was as if my brain was refusing to process the news and my heart was completely in shock. Something did not add up here. It felt like a lump in my throat, or maybe worse, yes, a lot worse, because I felt my throat closing to the point where I could not breath. And that was just the beginning. Was I supposed to cry? Scream?

I did not know how to react. My head was muddled with a million thoughts, none of them clear enough to comprehend. My limbs were weighed down with numbness. My heart ached. Not only emotionally, but physically as well. My heart and my head actually ached as sharp pains pierced them both. My eyes burnt. That is all I can say about the pain because I was literally at a loss for words. I could not grasp what the news was doing to me at that time. It was extremely difficult to understand it all in a matter of seconds. Honestly, I have no idea how I survived that day, pushed through it all, and kept myself together. I had been so certain this time, since the PGS results showed that one embryo was completely healthy and of a good quality (Grade A). So I was both emotionally and physically convinced that I would get a positive pregnancy test.

As we were heading home, I asked my husband if he could drop me off at my parents' house. I did not want to go home. I could not stand it. I could not stand myself, my skin, the air, the car, anything. I wanted to get out of the here and now. I wanted a void. An absolute void. I wanted no one and nothing. I just wanted to get it all off my chest because it was suffocating me this time, physically. I was gasping for air.

I told my mother what had happened, and asked if I could lie down in her room for a while without any disturbance. I dragged my feet one step after the other until I reached upstairs. I felt I was drained of energy, walking dead. The colors around me faded, and for the first time in my life I could not smell my mom's cooking mixed with her favorite lavender perfume. My hands were dry, and so was my throat. It was very difficult for me to swallow. My eyes ached when I blinked. The distance between the stairs and my parents' room never felt longer. The closer I got to the door, the further it seemed from me. Was I hallucinating? I placed both of my pale hands over the cold door handle and pushed the door open with whatever remaining energy I had left in my body. I had to push harder because the dark green carpet got stuck behind the door. It got stuck again and I started steaming up, so I kicked the door in an attempt to close it behind me because my weak hands failed me. Then I cried. I cried it all out until I had no tears left and my eyes burned. I yelled until I stopped hearing my own whisper. I lost my breath between the long sobs and gasps. After it all came out, I heard something like a buzzing sound in my ears and felt a terrible headache. I stopped, because I had nothing left to pour out. Nothing. I felt empty, and that is what I needed. Feeling nothing is sometimes required to start again. This entire "emptying" of everything inside of me I did alone. Sometimes, even my parents, who were my best therapists, or the man I loved and shared almost everything with, could not see me like this. It would hurt them too much, and they would never forget what they saw. People can take it up to certain limits. I have realized that there are phases in life that should be explored alone.

I knew God saved the best for last. Time would not make me forget, but it would heal me. One day, God willing, I would hold my grandchildren, surrounded by my children. I would look back with gratitude and say, "Thank God for this amazing blessing. Thank God for giving us the most precious gift of all. In the end, it happened. And we are together now, and that is all that really matters."

Sunshine in the City of Fog

The next two cycles were entirely different from the previous ones. We had to leave our country, family, friends, work, and everyone we knew, everything we were used to, and travel all the way to another part of the world. London, here we come!

I felt so blessed and thankful, because in my country, if a couple has had five or more unsuccessful IVF trials, they get an opportunity to travel abroad to choose from a list of the best doctors in the field of IVF from different countries. We are afforded the true privilege of getting a free trial for another round of IVF at the government's expense. This was such a blessing for us. We took it as a sign. God always has a better plan than the one we make for ourselves. We chose London. There, we met with the best doctor in the field of IVF, Dr. Yaqoub Khalaf, and his marvelous team.

*****

To Dr. Khalaf and his most amazing team: Thank God for putting you in our way. This was a true blessing and the winning chance any IVF couple would ask for.

To us, this was like winning the golden ticket to Willy Wonka's chocolate factory. When you read this, just know that my husband and I are so thankful for everything you did for us. Thank you for being kind. Thank you for being patient. Thank you for being so understanding.

I am so grateful for my beloved country for giving us the amazing opportunity to be under your care.

To all the stars I have encountered, without you, my sky would not have been as radiant.

*****

As soon as we got to London, we started the treatment immediately. The test results were amazing, things went freakishly smoothly, and we found a great apartment to stay in. It was two blocks from Harrods. Imagine that. We found a grocery store, Sainsbury's, the best! Coffee shops, McDonalds, an underground station, and a Boots pharmacy close by. That was not all, the famous Hyde Park was nearby too. Could it get any better? I didn't think so.

I got pregnant and I was so happy. I could not stay home; I wanted to see everything and everyone and eat everything. We started buying gifts for our families, even though I was so tired and the pregnancy signs started to show immediately. But I just could not lock myself in. I was just so happy. Did I mention that I started talking to my tummy? It was magical. We were living our own fairytale. My husband videoed our first ultrasound appointment after the pregnancy was confirmed and we heard our precious baby's heartbeat.

It was strong and beautiful. It was the best melody our ears had ever heard. Those moments were so magical that I wanted time to repeat itself over and over again. This sound gave me strength, hope, love and joy, and other feelings that words cannot come close to describing. Tears of joy do taste differently than tears of sadness, and they make your vision clearer instead of more blurry.

After the tenth week of pregnancy, right before the end of the first trimester, we had an appointment to check on the baby's growth. I remember Dr. Khalaf asking me when was the last time I felt nauseous, and I said that morning. He scrunched his face and started focusing on the monitor in a silence that stretched longer and louder with every tick of the round clock hanging on the wall. After a few minutes, he left the room without a word and called his colleague from the other diagnosis room at the opposite corridor to come and look at the ultrasound.

Worry took over. My body temperature rose and the place felt so hot and small that I started to sweat. The air was not enough for me to breathe properly, my ears and cheeks turned blood red, and my limbs were ice cold. I tried my very best to keep myself calm. I felt something was coming. Good or bad? I had no idea. Our doctor's colleague approached the computer screen and started zooming the results in and out and typing words and numbers. She pushed back her thick round glasses with shiny black plastic frames from her washed-out blue eyes and said, "I am sorry, dear, there is no heartbeat."

Our doctor said that it had just stopped, no longer than 24 to 48 hours earlier. I felt a sharp pain, and a little shock perhaps, but not like the other times. That made me wonder: Why? I mean, I had just been told that our baby was no longer alive. But I was not showing any reaction.

My husband was more shocked than I was. I saw it in his face, his eyes. He was struck by a blend of cutting emotions, sharper than an axe. They caused a deep wound. Was it fear of the truth in what had been said or disappointment or unexplained apprehension? The features of those particular emotions, which he was clearly trying to hold in and which I could not yet identify, created lines on his face until he let go completely. He was not able to hold back his tears this time. Every time in the past he would calm me down. But this time it was my turn. I did the best I could to hide my feelings and any expression so as not to compound his.

I honestly do not have a clue as to what had happened to me. I seriously was stronger than ever. My tightened, stressed muscles relaxed, like I had been given some sort of sedative drug. I was calm. For the first time in our IVF journey, I felt unbreakable. It wasn't like I didn't care anymore, but I just accepted it, the way it was. I did not ask any questions or comment on anything. I was not curious at all to know a single reason for the loss. I could not explain to myself what had happened to me. Had I gotten used to it? Had it become so easy for me that time would make me forget? Would the next time be better? Was I a good person because I just did not want to hurt myself more? Or was I a bad person because I just lost my baby and I could not grieve? Should I have been worried about my mental and emotional state at this stage? Should I tell someone about it at least, or keep talking to myself instead? Why was this happening to me? Had I gone insane? I could not find any answers to these questions.

I remember one thing I always used to remind myself of until I fully believed it. If it is meant to happen, it will happen. This belief became true. It became a part of me. I realized then that our sixth attempt was not meant to be. It was not our winning shot yet. Simply because there was no good in it, and because we deserved better, much better. I was certain of that. We believed something great was on the way. We would wait, and God willing, we would be amazed.

We spent almost three weeks waiting for the miscarriage to occur naturally. It did not happen and I did not bleed. Not even a drop. Until then, I had spent weeks taking so much care of this pregnancy that it had become my entire life. Now, I was just waiting for it to end as soon as possible. Did wanting this make me a bad person? I knew the baby was dead and keeping it inside could put my life at risk. But I still blamed myself for it. I did not know if wanting to get rid of a precious piece of me made me a terrible person, or shall I say a terrible mother? Rationally and medically, it was the right and only option, but my heart was resisting logic. I wished there were a way to keep my baby with me. It sounds insane, but I still considered myself a mother who refused to leave her baby behind and move on. Did I have the right at least to feel that way? Did I?

Our doctor decided to go for the dilation and curettage (D&C) option, a routine procedure to terminate pregnancies in the first trimester. This is how the sixth trial came to an end. It was not what I anticipated, at all, but it surely occurred for a reason. A good reason, yes, I believed it. My husband requested a full genetic analysis of the fetus. Four weeks later the results came back. The baby was completely normal and healthy. Life is just full of unexpected events. You will witness one, or maybe more, every single day.

I realized something significant after getting the analysis results back. Some reasons are meant to be hidden, for our own good and peace of mind. It is a way God shows mercy. That is how I interpret it. If God destines it to happen, it will. Regardless of all boundaries and uncertainties, regardless of all facts that we might sometimes view as obstacles, with God's will it will happen.

*****

Remember when I said we were so lucky and blessed? Well, we were. Even though we had the hardest times in these two trials because we were away from our home and our loved ones, something miraculous came out of them.

My husband and I spoke to our country's medical office in London asking for one more chance. After a series of long discussions and phone calls, in addition to the medical reports going back and forth like a ping pong in a professional tournament, somehow, we got the approval. This was another sign, and we held on to it as much as we could.

We decided to go for a fresh cycle and repeat the entire process all over again. Even though my body needed more rest from the previous cycle and miscarriage, I did not want to wait. I lack patience, and I am extremely stubborn, I am aware of that. I had this voice in my head telling me I must do it. I heard it every day. I did not know if I had gone crazy, but that voice was encouraging me so I didn't care.

On the freezing cold morning of February 18, 2017, two embryos were transferred to my uterus by my doctor's amazing colleague, Dr. Tarek. We waited for 10 days and after that I took a home pregnancy test. At dawn on February 28, I peed on the pregnancy test stick and shivered while waiting. My husband was praying in the living room. After about two minutes, I screamed so loudly that surely every neighbor heard me. Two lines, one strong and the other a little faint but clearly there. I was not hallucinating! I called out to my husband, and he joined me as soon as he finished his prayers. The look on his face was indescribable. It was worth a million words, I swear. He was walking on air. Happy is the least I could say about how we felt when we found out we were pregnant again.

We went for the first ultrasound appointment to check on the heartbeat, but it was too early to detect it. I was only five weeks pregnant. At the following appointment, I met my doctor to check for the heartbeat and the progress of the pregnancy and everything went well. There was only one embryo. The second one did not implant. But I focused on the bright side. There was one and it was healthy. We requested a harmony blood test (to detect any genetic abnormalities and determine the baby's gender). The tests were sent to Los Angeles for analysis. Two weeks later, I received a phone call from the lab. Thank God, the results were normal, and it was a baby girl! My husband was not home when the lab called. He had to finish up some paperwork before we left the city of fog. So I texted him to reassure him the baby was completely healthy and not carrying any genetic disease. Instead of revealing the gender of the baby right away, I decided to play a little game. I wrote a series of notes, each with a clue on it. I distributed them all over the house: one in the fridge, another in the oven, one in the frying pan and one taped to my belly! The very last step was to open the note application on my phone. His eyes lit up with pure joy when he found out that we would be adding a princess to our little family.

We decided to keep the pregnancy just between us until we passed the first trimester. I had weekly appointments for ultrasounds. I knew it was not necessary to go so often but it just made me feel better and more reassured. I would freak out when I felt cramps and go crazy when I got up not feeling morning sickness. I had cravings for sour foods, cheddar cheese, and, of course, my number one favorite, freshly squeezed bitter orange juice. I would smell a garlic scent on my husband right before we went to bed and fight with him to eat garlic-flavored hummus.

They were good days with many crazy, yet special memories. With the first trimester safely behind us, it was time to return home.

My Own Path Forward

We booked flights for May 2, 2017, to go back to our lovely home and beautiful families. The day of our flight, we were still waiting for our passports to head to the airport. We had had to renew our visas (our visas were only valid for six months). The procedure was long and complicated, with lots of paperwork, but my darling husband took care of that. As we waited, the medical office called and informed us that our passports were lost. From 8 am, my heroic husband started running a marathon from the medical office in Kensington, to the visa office in Shepherd's Bush, to the post office in who knows where, using all available subways during rush hour, trying desperately to find an answer. After hours of long prayers and running everywhere with dozens of calls to everyone we knew in the embassy and medical office, it was discovered that the front desk employee in the medical office accidentally took the delivered package that included our passports and put it in the storeroom without opening it. However, a really kind and dedicated team from the medical office helped us to trace the package and miraculously thought of searching the storeroom to find it (no one had suggested that before, because it almost never happened). This was the power of honest prayer: it worked wonders. This was what I called real-life action.

Passports in hand, we were ready to head to Heathrow Airport, one of the most hectic and crowded airports in the world, with queues everywhere and hundreds of people waiting. Luckily, that was not the case for us. There are always benefits to being pregnant. We got to the airport three hours before our departure time. I barely found a seat so I could rest while my husband was hustling in the check-in point. When it was our turn to check in I mentioned that I was a high-risk pregnancy patient and could not wait in all the lines. I asked for a wheelchair, and was given it, along with an upgrade. After the check-in point, things went perfectly smoothly. I am truly grateful for the consideration and empathy I received, and wish more pregnant women received it in public places. No one truly knows what a toll it takes on a woman to carry a miracle, whether it is a normal pregnancy or otherwise. In any case, a pregnant woman is growing another human inside of her so these small considerations make things just a bit easier.

My husband called my parents to break the happy news. My father picked up the phone first. My husband said, "I have two pieces of good news. The first is that we are having a baby and we have passed the first trimester successfully! The second is that we are in the airport right now and we'll hopefully be home tomorrow morning." My father started to cry, we could tell from his voice before we even finished breaking the news to him. My mother was over the moon.

We then called a few others in our close family circle but wanted to keep the pregnancy low profile. That was my decision. I did not want to feel any external pressure. I felt it was best to keep it like that. It felt right for me. After a series of happy and excited phone calls, we relaxed in the first-class lounge. I had a banana and some chicken biryani. I could not miss the privilege of being in the first-class lounge and just have a banana and some fresh orange juice!

We had a very comfortable night flight. The one remaining obstacle was the toilet. I hate using public toilets, especially airplane toilets. I just can't stand them. When I was forced to use the toilet, it took me a decade of cleaning and sanitizing before using it. I used it only once and thank God I did not have to use it again during that night flight. We landed with the first light of day, which was a good thing because the airport was not crowded at all, and that is what we really needed. We wanted to get home fast.

Shortly after landing, I called my grandmother. "Granny, we are finally here!" I said. She could not speak. She was so happy. She cried so hard! I was a little surprised, because I always see my grandmother as the strong and independent woman who raised eight children by herself because when she was only 27 years old my grandfather passed away due to cancer. She is my idol. I am her first grandchild and I am truly proud to be. Here is one funny fact about her: She still gives me money for food and gas, because she still sees me as the grand kid who will never grow up. I will always be her precious little one. She is now a successful businesswoman even though she did not finish her education. She insisted that all her children get a college degree to have a better life. She succeeded. From her, I learned to fight my way through to stay alive. From her, I learned that the harder it gets, the stronger I become and the closer I get to my dreams.

*****

Grandma Eva: I love you. I believe these few words are not nearly enough to tell the world about you. You are one of a kind. A fighter, a mother, my idol. Your presence makes us happy and strong, and your voice brings us all together, always.

*****

Two weeks later, I was staying at my parents' place. I awoke late one Friday morning to the sweet aroma of my mother's food. I surrendered. My mom served a late yet delicious homemade breakfast in their newly furnished dining room. All my favorite dishes were right in front of me. My mom served the breakfast in her exquisite yellow and gold table set. She doesn't serve food in that particular set unless there is a special occasion. I had seen this set in what she called "big special events" only. I was spoiled and pampered for sure. The huge mahogany table had all the options a royal breakfast would include, a wide selection of food from all continents. There were all kinds of manakish (a popular

Levantine food similar to pizza consisting of dough topped with cheese or za'atar (thyme) or spiced ground beef), cooked beans and four kinds of eggs: omelet, scrambled, sunny-side up and boiled. Mom had to boil those eggs for 15 minutes because she knew it would make me feel better that way. Runny eggs were on the forbidden list during pregnancy. There was an indulgent selection of freshly baked bread. The smell of the moist, puffy sour dough beat every smell I knew in my entire life. There were at least four kinds of olives of different shades and flavors and my Nutella jar (one teaspoon per day was my daily indulgence). My favorite dip, hummus, freshly squeezed orange juice, chopped tomato and cucumber, crispy golden brown deep-fried falafel pieces, oatmeal and cereals with my favorite dried fruits, a hot teapot of English breakfast tea and karak tea. I honestly cannot remember the rest, because I was busy loading my empty stomach with whatever my hands and eyes could reach. We chatted about baby names, preparations for the delivery and my plans afterward.

At around 11:00 am, right after our lovely breakfast came to an end, I felt something strange. A familiar feeling: the feeling of bleeding. I excused myself and went to the guest room. I could not walk the stairs to my regular room on the first floor, so I was staying in the guest room temporarily. I checked, and my suspicions were confirmed. I started having some brown discharge just like when my period starts. I tried to calm myself down as much as I could. A few minutes later, it started spotting. It then turned to fresh red blood. I rushed to the toilet immediately. I started bleeding heavily. I grabbed whatever small towels I could from the wooden cabinet to avoid making a mess. The bleeding increased, and the towels failed to absorb all the blood. I shifted my wobbling body as slowly as I could to the shower. The warm blood spurted between my legs, soaking my feet more and more. Was the blood mine or the baby's? I did not know. I hoped it was me and not the baby. My vision blurred and I could no longer focus on anything around me: everywhere I looked I saw red. My heartbeat reached the tip of my throat and ears. Bloody footprints and handprints multiplied around the white tiles and stained the silver faucet. The metallic odor of crimson was heavy in the air and pervaded my nostrils. The shower floor became very slippery. A sudden sharp chill took root in every bone and nerve in my body. I searched for something sturdy to lean my shivering, half-dressed body on. In the shower, warm water, blood and a river of burning salty tears mixed together.

I shouted for my mom. After a couple of times, I realized that my voice wouldn't come out. The accumulated water vapor in the small glass box had me choking; I felt like I was suffocating blindly with the walls closing in on me. I held tight to the shower's metal door handle to avoid slipping, because I started getting dizzy as the bleeding continued. One last time, I screamed at the top of my lungs, "Mother, save me please!" She was the only person I could think of. She was the only person who could see me in that state. I heard her footsteps running towards the toilet and pushing the door open.

When she saw the amount of blood gushing out of me, I can only imagine what she thought. It was a sight that no mother should see: her daughter cowering, fear etched on her face, blood everywhere. She froze in her tracks, as if entering a catatonic state. Not blinking, not moving, not breathing, and not knowing the source of the blood. Her only movement after what seemed like an eternity was her delicate hand reaching out to the edge of the sink to balance her frozen body. Speechless and confused, it seemed like she was carefully weighing the options about what she should do before it was too late for her child and her grandchild. Would she lose them both? Could she move her petrified body? Could she speak? Could she do anything?

Just when I thought she would stand there frozen forever, she ran out. Later I would learn that with trembling hands she attempted time and time again to call my husband on her cell phone, unable to recall the number she had dialed hundreds of times before. She recalled how the bright light of the screen had blurred her vision, making her unable to dial a digit of the number. It was only when another scream of mine snapped her to her senses and freed her from paralysis that she could phone my husband to come and pick us up right away. Luckily, I lived 30 seconds away from my parents' house, and that helped a lot.

From where we were, we could hear the reassuring growl of my husband's Dodge Ram engine signaling that help was on the way. My mom washed my red-stained clothes and wiped all the blood off the bathroom in a matter of minutes and helped me put some dry clothes on. She grabbed my right arm tightly and led me to the living room sofa, stretched my legs forward, resting my back slightly on the cushions, and tucked a small pillow under my knees. She said the position would help rest my body and control the bleeding a little bit. She combed my messy hair and put my shoes on for me.

After she had dressed me, I gingerly took steps to exit the house and to the car door. I refused to let go of her hands and insisted that she escort me to the ER. She had six successful pregnancies and two miscarriages. She knew a lot and her experience would help for sure. Every minute was critical. Every second made a difference. Friday is a holiday in our country and it was still before noon, so the streets were mostly empty. My husband stepped on the gas to the max. The empty streets echoed with the shriek of the Ram's engine. The high-pitched, ear-splitting sound the machine made every time he hit the gas shook our insides like a child shaking out a box of biscuits, eager to reach every last crumb. It usually takes us 20 minutes to get to the nearest hospital. But with a little bit of fast and furious drifts along the way, we got there in five minutes. That was a record indeed.

At the hospital, a couple of patients were ahead of me. My mom had me sit down on a plastic chair next to the vital signs room and took my health card and approached the front desk to register my information and get a number.

I could not identify the emotional state I was in. It was like a door had been slammed in my face. Was it numbness, apathy, fear or shock? I had a sick feeling in the pit of my stomach and I could not think straight. Colors faded. Only black and white remained. The voices and sounds were forcing their way through my head, conquering my brain. I wished for silence. I wished to be swallowed by a void. I wanted to press fast forward and end this chaos, once and for all. Forever. I wanted to breathe, just breathe in. Something was choking me, sucking all the air around me, and leaving me in an abandoned place. Without any directions or anyone to ask. I saw walls. No doors or windows existed. It struck so bad this time. It hurt when I breathed, it hurt when I blinked, and it hurt every time my heart beat.

When my number lit up on the screen I was called into the examination room without my mother. Only patients were allowed in, without relatives, no matter how close. I told the nurse what had happened and when, in detail. The nurse asked me to show her the sanitary pad I was wearing so she could note the quantity and color of the bleeding as she typed in the diagnosis. After this many rounds of IVF, having had doctors and nurses poke and prod me, seeing me in my most vulnerable physical and emotional states, a request like this no longer shocked or disgusted me. I simply complied cooperatively.

The pad was nearly clean. Only three dull spots stained the pad. She gave me a silly look as if I was lying or kidding, breathed, nodded and continued typing. My eyes glistened, my voice rose and my face wrinkled.

"I swear I am not lying. I almost drowned myself in my own blood at home. I am not here on a holiday to ask for two days' sick leave, and I am not here to pretend that I am sick. Please write that I had heavy bleeding, and a panic attack, or else I am not leaving this spot for the rest of the day," I said.

She tried to interrupt but I insisted I was not being overdramatic and requested an ultrasound examination on the spot. "We cannot get you in straight away, and you need a vaginal examination first," she answered.

My tears burst forth like water from a dam, my face turned crimson and my fists hardened. I stretched to my full height. "I want an ultrasound now," I said with clenched teeth. "I am not going to lose this one too. Do you understand me? I am not doing any vaginal examination." I gathered the last dose of energy I had and added, "I cannot afford to lose this baby now. Please help."

I tucked in my shirt, wiped the tears off my cheeks, left the examining room and took my seat again in the waiting hall. Thank God my mother and husband were there with me. I needed company to lift the heavy burden with me, someone to talk to and keep me distracted. A lot of dark and crazy thoughts were going through my mind and I could not handle one more issue. My mother always told me to refuse a vaginal examination. Thank God she told me that before this happened.

A nurse called my name 15 minutes later and asked me to wait in the ultrasound waiting area, which was located in a neighboring wing. A young female Sudanese doctor asked me to lay on the bed. She was the only doctor on call that day. She dimmed the lights of the examination room and covered my legs up to my hips with a white bed sheet. She asked me to uncover my baby bump while she input my information and processed my urgent ultrasound request. After pouring the warmed transparent gel on my belly, she moved the transducer across my baby bump, right to left and up and down several times. She pressed a little harder at certain points. "Please doctor, find something, anything, I beg of you," I pleaded, staring at the ultrasound monitor, not blinking, holding my breath, and grabbing the sheet so tightly that my fingers whitened and started to feel numb. My ears were steaming hot and my feet trembled continuously. Sweat beads covered my entire back and soaked my shirt.

After gazing and typing endlessly for five seemingly never-ending minutes, she put her right hand on my right thigh and gently patted me. She whispered, "The baby is fine, darling, stop panicking or you will hurt yourself and your precious one too."

She turned on the sound system a little so I could hear the heartbeat. I took a deep breath, and smiled until my cheeks hurt. "When did you last eat? Your baby is supposed to be moving at this time of day," the doctor said.

My lips flattened a bit, my eyes widened and I straightened my back and sat on the edge of the bed. "Is the baby tired? Is the baby hungry? Please, is there something wrong now?" I shot out my questions like bullets, one after the other.

"Go eat something. Your baby needs food to move a little. It was just vaginal bleeding, in case you wanted to know. No threat to the baby, but you need bed rest until the bleeding stops entirely, and eat food rich in iron. You lost too much blood and your body needs fuel, Mama," the doctor replied.

It seemed impossible: I had just finished breakfast when the pain started. I had indulged in it all, not sparing a morsel … or had I? I remember laughing and chatting with my mom, dreaming of the baby inside of me while eating. Or was I just pecking at my food, tasting a bite here and a bite there? The nurse had me questioning whether I had in fact gotten enough nourishment during breakfast so I grabbed my things and jetted out of the room, trying to remember where I had seen the nearest vending machine.

The baby needed food and that was the only concern that conquered my thoughts and attention. I did not even remember to call my husband to deliver the good news until after I found the vending machine. I inserted whatever cash my mom had in her purse without counting and punched whatever numbers my eyes could see. I got some canned orange juice, roasted peanuts and chocolate-filled biscuits. I knew it wasn't nourishing but I needed sugar first to kick start both of our energy levels. I found a place to sit and opened up everything I got. One hand shoved the food in my mouth and the other hand stayed on my belly, waiting for my star to tell me what she thought about the food. We felt relief.

For the rest of the pregnancy, I glued myself to the bed and sofa. Whenever I needed to shop for the baby, I did it in a wheelchair.

*****

In the end, my husband and I decided to keep the pregnancy low profile throughout. Some close family members thought that it was unnecessary to do that, and that I was being a little too cautious. I did it for reasons that made sense to me, and I think that is reason enough.

Everyone experiences pregnancy differently, and when you are an IVF patient that adds yet another layer. I noticed that many people would talk about their pregnancy experiences negatively. They did it with good intentions, trying to warn me of things that I did not even know about in the first place, and trying to pass on their knowledge. They would give long speeches with a list of do's and don'ts, almost 90% of which were just myths. Or it might have happened to one pregnant woman, and she thought now it would happen to everyone else. It was absolutely fine for some people to listen and engage in this kind of talk without being influenced, but for me the situation was different. Sometimes when I heard these things I would get nervous and start overthinking and begin the never-ending process of research on whether this or that harmed the pregnancy. For example, someone told me that eating dates made women go into labor. And that eating lemon causes bleeding during the early stages of pregnancy. And that pineapple could lead to miscarriage. Why would I put myself through this if I could avoid it? I wanted peace of mind, that was all.

Additionally, no matter how hard I tried to put the experience of fertility treatment into words, some people didn't seem to understand it. When I said I was an IVF patient, and that was why I was a little bit more careful with my pregnancy, I received annoying comments. For example, "You are not the only one who has done IVF," or "Some people are in greater pain than you are right now." This was true, some people suffer far more than I did, and it is also true that I am not the first or last person in the world who has had to go through IVF to conceive.

But there is something really important that people with such attitudes should be aware of before making these reckless comments. IVF is physically and emotionally grueling. I shed blood and tears. I underwent hundreds of painful vaginal ultrasounds and had blood tests every other morning during an IVF cycle. I had painful ovarian stimulation hormone therapy, sometimes two or three injections per day, and suffered bruises and burns from the injections. Once the medicine went in, I felt like cutting my skin to let it out and breathe. My abdomen swelled, not with child but with foreign substances that caused painful bloating and cramps, and my entire body changed. I suffered extraordinary mood swings. I had to undergo full anesthesia for every egg collection. I had to hold my breath and suck in all the pain during every embryo transfer procedure because it is done without sedation. During embryo transfer, a tool is used to hold the vagina and cervix wide open and a catheter is then inserted all the way in until it reaches the womb where the embryos are finally released. And all of this, which takes at least 40 minutes, has to be done on a full bladder. There is a vaginal suppository twice a day during the two-week wait, which is sometimes extended depending on the case of the patient.

Many people suffer worse than I did, I am certain of that. I am not the only IVF patient in the world, that is correct too. But people who say these things in fact haven't walked my path to judge me. They haven't been through the psychological hurt and the physical breakdown when an IVF round fails. It hurts more than words can describe, trust me. Even as I try to explain all that I went through here, in the pages of this book, I feel my words fall short. People were never easy on me when I took the decision to undergo in vitro fertilization, so why would I subject myself to their fear mongering and opinions during my pregnancy?

Before you start judging people, step into their shoes and see how it feels to walk their path.

The Miracle Arrives

The day we had been waiting for started like this. On October 1, 2018, at 5:35 am, I suffered from a leakage. That means the baby's water started leaking, but my uterus was fully closed and there was no pain yet to signal contractions, and my water did not break. I went to the hospital at 8:00 am and was examined. I was expecting to be home after an hour or so. I thought it would just be a checkup. The ER doctor said, "You are suffering from a leakage. You cannot leave. Your water did not break yet and you could get an infection. It is dangerous for both you and the baby. If you do not go into labor in the next few hours, we will have to induce."

That was a lot of information to receive in a short amount of time. But all I chose to understand was that I would meet my little one soon. That was all that mattered to me.

I was admitted and given an antibiotic to prevent any chance of getting an infection because of the leakage. Then, I was induced. I was told the medicine that would be used looked exactly like a suppository. Well, it did not. It looked like a pill, a small oval yellow pill that looked like any pain killer. Believe it or not, the way this medication was given hurt more than egg collection, embryo transfer and any physical vaginal examination I had ever experienced. The pill had to be physically placed at the tip of the cervix. The pain was incomparable. It felt like a sharp knife cutting through my flesh in slow motion, followed by a severe burn like that dragging pain when lemon juice or salt meets an open wound. All in the most sensitive area of my body. Any movement my trembling swollen legs made, and any air my lungs inhaled, elevated the pain to a new level. It took the doctor only a few seconds to insert the medicine but it felt like a decade of Medieval torture. I grabbed the cold metal edges of the bed so tightly that my hands started to sweat and the IV almost tore up my vein due to excessive pressure. My heart was about to explode. The lower part of my body began to twitch uncontrollably, and then it froze. I could not help furiously grabbing a handful of the wet white blanket (I guess my water broke once the medicine was inserted, and it started soaking the bed sheet), kicked the bed and arched my back until my neck was about to break. I could not hold still. I tried. Tears and sweat drenched the gown I was wearing. Furious tears poured from my eyes and I screamed until I was hoarse.

The first dose had a minimal effect on my body. The second (and thankfully, last) dose had the required effect. The labor pain I had read about and heard a lot of women talk about started right after the second dose.

To be exact, five minutes after the second dose was given to me, a cramp like no other that I had ever felt before in my entire life hit me like a typhoon. It happened again five minutes later. The time interval shrunk from five to three minutes. And cramps is not even the right word to describe this pain that coursed through every fiber of my being. The worst and most painful period cramps cannot compare to labor contractions. It was not only abdominal pain; it was like my entire body was in a state of war. Every bone ached, my eyes burned, my lungs couldn't catch up with my breathing, my veins were tightened, and I pressed so hard on my teeth that one of my molars almost broke.

The midwife asked to perform a physical examination to check for cervix dilation. I screamed, "No, you're not, and get your hands off me right now!" I couldn't even see her face. I barely heard her voice. They transferred me to the delivery room. It was bright white and extremely cold. All I remember seeing was an incubator for the baby to be put in and silver blades of all kinds and sizes, and smelling a terrible sterilized scent that made me want to throw up.

The midwife and the nurse were engaged in a back-and-forth of medical terms that I couldn't keep up with, typing away furiously on the computer all the while, leaving me on the bed behind them begging for any kind of sedation to help survive what I had got myself into. I was planning to go for a drug-free delivery but once I encountered the true pain of it, the plan changed. But the medical team refused to give me any kind of sedation because the baby was premature, and it might pose a risk for her. So, I had to stick to plan A and naturally (and quite literally) push my way through. I have no idea how long labor lasted, because every time I looked at the clock, time hadn't changed at all. At 11:30 pm, the pain reached its peak, the tears stopped, I heard no voices or sounds, and there was just a bright light. All I heard was the nurse saying, "She is 9 cm dilated." I don't know if it was her words or it was time but right after she said that I felt an urge to push harder than any time in my life. Without saying a single word, I pulled off the wrinkled white bed sheet and pushed for the first time.

"Wait, don't push! The doctor is on her way," the nurse said, and attempted to re-cover my lower body. I furiously pushed away the sheet. I felt an even stronger urge for a bigger push. I pushed harder. A young female doctor (probably in her early 30's) with blonde hair, green eyes and a soft voice came in. She wore gloves and a mask and immediately cheered loudly and encouraged me to push, and push hard.

"One more push, Mama, and wait a second. Yes. Good job, Mama, your little star is officially here." Her words were the first thing my daughter heard.

Baby Bee (her nickname) was born on October 2, 2017, at 11:42 pm. She did not even cry.

I saw her cute little back but not her face, and she was taken away immediately for neonatal care because her blood sugar was low and the room was just too cold. She needed to be fed and placed in an incubator at exactly

37.5 degrees Celsius to maintain her weight and body temperature. I had no clue that newborns lose weight if they get placed in a cold environment. She weighed 1.9kg. Even though she was out already, my legs wouldn't stop shivering 10 minutes later. Twelve hours of labor. Yes, 12 hours of pain and tears and screams. I never imagined pain like this existed. Mothers all over the world must be appreciated. What they do is never easy. The experience was a combination of terror, pain, happiness and action. It simply had it all.

Ten minutes later, my husband came in, holding our tiny precious princess in his hands. He was the first one to hold her. I was jealous! He gently put her in my hands. I was sweaty, shivering and very tired, but when I saw her face, the pain disappeared, I swear. It was the most incredible moment I have ever lived in my entire life. Nothing could compete with it, ever. It was what I shed blood, sweat and tears for. It was what I handled all kinds of pain for. It was magical. It was beautiful, in every sense of the word. We were blessed. If I had to go through it all again, I would do it. I would not mind bearing the pain again for this.

Her delicate face glowed from within. That dear little thing had the beautiful, dark hazel, almond-shaped eyes of her father, but definitely my long thin eyebrows – straight as an arrow. Her soft gaze could melt even the hardest of hearts, which my husband jokes is common to us both. For the first few days, she had my same soft vanilla skin tone with ever-blushing cheeks, just like her grandfather. Crowning her head was a mess of deep brown hair. When she reached her tiny fingers to my face as I held her close to my heart, she was mirroring the way I held my father's face as a child. I would learn later as she grew into a happy, healthy baby and then a toddler that she had my stubborn spirit and would always get her way no matter what. But at that moment, she was just my miracle in the flesh. She was an amazing combination of what I loved in myself and what I loved in her father. My heart swelled with love for both.

I did not want to show too much affection between me and her in front of everyone. Yes, the delivery room was very crowded. My husband, my mother and my aunt were there, in addition to the medical staff. I wanted to spend some time alone with my baby. Finally, I could say "my own baby," and not worry about someone else holding her or feeding her or taking her away.

Despite the crowd, the noise and the distractions, I saw something in her eyes. I gazed, in complete amazement. It was not merely my reflection. In her eyes, I saw my true self. In her eyes, I saw a miracle. In her eyes, my soul witnessed something beyond love. It was not a bond like they always say. It was two souls braided together perfectly. How do you explain holding a precious dream in your hands? How do you describe holding a blessing so close to your heart, alive and breathing? These words, even as I write them, are inept in explaining a fraction of what I felt at the time. It was a feeling that left an unexplainable expression on my face. A smile drawn on the face only when remembering moments like those. Moments that will forever be imbedded in the memory of my life.

*****

I was famished after the delivery. I could have eaten an entire cow. Or maybe two. I craved Indian food so badly. I wanted to order extra spicy chicken biryani with extra garlic and onion on top, yoghurt salad on the side, and three giant pieces of nan butter bread, extra crispy, extra butter. I wanted chickpea curry, three golden sweet and juicy ras malai and saffron ice cream topped with pistachios for dessert. After making this list in my head, I realized it was 2:00 am, and most of the decent Indian restaurants were closed. There was one chapati and poori canteen that I used to crave and go to during my pregnancy. Luckily, it was open 24/7. My husband got me two family-sized chapati, 12 inches each and loaded with extra cream cheese. I did not have time to wash my hands. I pushed my messy hair behind my ears and held both chapatis, one in the left hand and one in the right. I centered myself in the bed, pulled the sheets away, stretched my legs, sat up straight and in full attention, tore open the aluminum foil clumsily with my already full hands and threw it behind me. I wolfed down the first chapati in three minutes and swallowed the second one whole. I do not remember chewing any of the bites. The melted cheese covered my lips and I looked like I was wearing a shade of matte lipstick. The cheese dripped between my fingers like maple syrup. My white gown was covered in thin golden brown crisps of greasy chapati mixed with melted cheese. I was amazed by the amount of food my body consumed in one shot. They always say, "Do not mess or speak with a hungry woman!" That is very true. Honestly, I felt there was room for a third chapati with just a little bit of Nutella (this special occasion called three full tablespoons, I think!).

*****

The first person I called after my delivery was my best friend. She had no clue I was pregnant. She picked up the call, and I said, "Hey, I know it's late, but I have to tell you something important. I just gave birth to a baby girl." She was a little shocked, but what stunned me was that she did not hang up on me. She is my best friend and I thought she would be mad for not telling her about something this important. She knew about my IVF journey and about the London medical trip. Later, I asked her this question many times. I said, "Aren't you mad because I hid it from you all that time, and we're not only best friends, but sisters?"

She sighed, looked me in the eye and said, "Look, I know you, you hid it for a reason. I know you better than anyone else. I understand what you have been through, and I know your personality. You are my best friend, and I accept you for who you are."

Am I not the luckiest person ever? Who gets a friend like her these days? Really, I was not expecting that at all. She has shocked me every day with her kindness, appreciation, love, support and prayers.

My beloved friend A: I thank God every day for having you in my life. You are a true gift, or shall I say, a blessing? You are both.

*****

My room in the hospital was even better than expected. I dreamt of this room way before I decided to become a mother or even got married. Whenever I visited new parents in the hospital, I used to imagine myself resting in that cozy white bed filled with puffy pillows and a soft white blanket. I imagined holding my own baby close to my heart, singing "Twinkle, Twinkle, Little Star" in a soft voice and whispering, "I love you, my precious one." I have had this scene in my head for years. And every time I imagined this scene I tried to add some new touches to it and make it better than the previous time.

When my turn finally came, my husband booked me a VIP room. My room had the most perfect decoration. It was more like a guest suite at a French country manor. The walls were painted in peach with some matte gold and dark wooden details and engraved with baby roses and leaves that glistened in the light. To the left of the bed there was an arch that led to a small pantry to prepare hot drinks and beverages. Behind the pantry was a floor-to-ceiling window that allowed for bright sunlight, and breath-taking sunrise and sunset views. There was a wood table with a beige and gold marble top, and a 70-inch Blu-ray TV screen and a full intercom system. There was space for chocolate trays, flower vases and gifts. There were built-in hand-crafted glass shelves with golden edges where I placed the white and peach peonies in a Villeroy and Boch vase that my mom brought me. The background of the glass shelves had a delicate hidden lighting system that turned the shelves into a gleaming antiquity when lit. There was a large L-shaped sofa that could accommodate at least six people, which was a soothing shade of beige with pale pistachio. There were two extra olive green armchairs placed at both ends of the sofa in case more visitors decided to come in all at once, which happened all the time.

My mother bought me a new pink bed set with extra puffy pillows to support my back, a matching tulle robe and flip flops, a baby pink handmade wooden antique clock, a pink rabbit-shaped lamp, and, believe me when I say it, balloons in every shape and size. She reserved the best café service for the guests in town from 10 am to 9 pm during my whole stay in the hospital. She also bought trays of the finest, smoothest and most delicious Swiss chocolate in town: Läderach, of course. I ate whatever my stomach could stand. Milk chocolate, dark chocolate, chocolate truffles, chocolate-coated biscuits, caramel-filled chocolate, strawberry-filled chocolate, hazelnut cream, almond and Brazilian nut chunks. You name it, I ate it! Like an addiction, whatever I did to get away from it, it found its way back to me. That pure fresh cocoa smell called to me seductively. Chocolate was not just food for me at that point. It fueled my engines. Every soft, thin layer was a world of wonder waiting to be explored and savored, and I loved the exotic way it melted in my mouth. Certain flavors took me back in time and allowed me to recall some of my most precious childhood memories. It was not the first time in my life eating chocolate, but I stopped eating it when I was pregnant to avoid any chance of developing gestational diabetes or increasing the caffeine levels in my blood (eight months seems like forever without those cocoa cubes of happiness). I read and had been told that too much caffeine might hurt the baby and was somehow linked to miscarriage. So during pregnancy, I had very few pieces to satisfy a fraction of my huge, wild craving for it. Right after my little sunshine hit the exit door, chocolate found its path to my mouth.

I stayed in the hospital for almost a week. Usually it is not that long, but my daughter was premature, so she stayed in the incubator for eight days, and I refused to leave the hospital even though I knew she was in good hands. I used to stay in the NICU for long hours, just watching her breathe and move slightly, and for some kangaroo care sessions (the best), when I would hold her against my skin. My mother and other family members took care of the guests when I was with her. Only a few people were allowed to visit the baby in the incubator. The parents could come at any time. The grandparents could come only once. Yes, it was that strict! I tried to breast feed her but her jaws were too weak to latch. I pumped the milk instead and fed her that way. Before entering the NICU, you must put on a sterilized gown, hair net and shoe covers, and wash your hands and sterilize them. I had to wash my breast every time I pumped milk to prevent any kind of bacteria or perfume from going into the baby's milk. All newborns have very sensitive digestive systems, and a premature baby has an even more delicate digestive system due to the lack of or incomplete formation of digestive enzymes and the stomach.

She was tiny, slightly bigger than my hands, like a squirrel. Her father and I watched her for hours and never got bored. Hugging a dream is a feeling that can never be explained. I would say it is like watching the beautiful sky on a warm summer night. Your eyes try to create a grid of the brightest star you can see. When your neck gets sore, you look down and find the most luminous moon in the galaxy resting between your hands, igniting some sort of a magical feeling in your soul.

I started writing this book on October 4, 2015, and had my baby on October 2, 2017. Almost exactly two years apart. If I knew then what I know now, I would have enjoyed every single moment I wasted in grief.

Only God knows everything I have been through. I risked my health and bore a lot of physical and emotional distress. I was stubborn and made the impossible happen; I advocated for my own health and care when faced with people or medical professionals who stood in my way. But it was worth it. I remind myself of the beautiful end, of the eight fascinating months of pregnancy and the miracle of birth, of the moment we saw each other for the first time, when our tears and heartbeats became one. I do not mind bearing the most painful procedure if the result is you. Whenever I fall, I will get up again, for our family.

Our kisses, cuddles and tears of joy, mixed with a touch of faith and grace, were the perfect ending to our story.

My Road to You

The following pages are dedicated to my future children, my dear readers and all IVF patients around the world. These words have made it easier for me to climb the high forts of despair to witness the beautiful sunrise of hope, as its warm golden rays cuddled the dewy red rose petals of faith.

To my snow-white lilies
My aurora lights in the dark nights
Here is what your mother wrote while anticipating you.
Every word I write is a lesson life taught me.
Read them.
Learn from them.

Tears of Hope

They think tears are a symbol of weakness.
I think tears are a window to the soul.
They say tears are an expression of pain.
I say it rains to make beautiful rainbows.
They shed tears when they are apart.
I cry to get closer to you.
Their tears blur their vision and make things fade to gray.
Mine draw a magnificent image of you in the chapters of my destiny.
When we one day meet, crystal beads from my radiant eyes will roll down your soft cheeks.
Then you will feel how much love I carried for you within every single heartbeat.
The moment we first meet will forever be engraved in my memory, not bound to any scale of time. It will be a redemption from dystopia, a new dimension created by our unity in a world, a moment you and I will both call a happily ever after.

Your Beat Is My Addiction

If patience is my gateway to you,
I beautifully will wait.
If pain is what I must encounter so we can cuddle,
I will push myself to the furthest limit and bear it.
If prayers make us meet, and I am certain they will,
I will pray every single moment until I see the two lines.

You complete the ultimate trio: you, your father, me.

You are what my heart terribly wants, my mind addictively needs, and my soul strongly desires.

Setbacks, sorrows and hate will raise their walls high, yet they can never prevent our dawn of hope from spreading its golden rays in the sky of tomorrow.

Although the pain I feel within right now cannot be rated on any kind of human scale, my wish to have you exceeds the horizons and surpasses all limits.

Simply because it is a need that only you can fulfill.

I Want

I want to wake up at midnight feeling your soft, tickling kicks against my belly.

I want to hear your sweet cries in the middle of the day, and hurry up to hold you tight and safe in my arms.

I want to dash off to baby shops and buy you cute baby outfits that say "I am Mummy's Hero" and "Cute Like Daddy."

I want to go to the supermarket, and head first to the baby food section, and then to the diapers.

I want, during family gatherings, to be able to participate when mothers my age talk about their amazing parenting experiences.

I want, when it is bed time and I can barely keep my eyes open, for a tiny finger to poke my sleepy head and whisper with a soft voice, "Mummy, Mummy, can I sleep next to you tonight?"

I want to attend your first day of kindergarten and your college graduation.

I want to attend your wedding and meet my grandchildren.

I want to have you.

Patience

I've been wondering for quite a long time why bad things happen to good people. And I think I have found the answer that I am looking for. There is always a bright side. Good things happen to those who wait.

Though sometimes our destiny makes us pay with great loss, it also pays us back, more than we can expect. Much more.

Patience. It is all about patience. Learn how to master it, and live happily. No matter how long it takes, if it is meant to be, it will hopefully be. Not at the time you want it to be, but when you need it the most and only God knows when that is. Never stop praying, because when one door closes, another one opens.

A human being cannot grasp the meaning of true happiness without experiencing the brutal effect of grief.

After all, you have to wait all night in the dark to witness the beautiful light of a dawning sunrise.

The Hardest Things

The hardest things are …

~ When people ask me to hold their newborn babies to see how beautiful they are, and I pretend not to know how to carry a baby when I do it better than they do. I am just afraid I will break down in front of them, that's all.

~ When we gather for a friend's wedding and I accidentally sit at a table where everyone is pregnant and has adorable baby bumps. The waiter comes and asks if we need anything, and each one of them asks for something they are craving, while I mutter to myself, "Can I have a baby, please?"

~ When relatives come over to my home with their kids. Every child sits beside their mother during lunch and the seat next to mine remains empty.

~ When, during family gatherings and holidays, someone asks, "What are you guys waiting for? When do you guys want to have a baby?" I say with a perfect smile and a heavy laugh that hides a broken heart and a typhoon of tears, "Oh! It's too early to have one! Why all the rush?"

~ When people around me start talking about the beauty of pregnancy and birth. I start making unnecessary phone calls, check Instagram just to keep myself busy and try to hide my face. It can easily be read.

~ When my period is a couple of weeks late and I dash off to any supermarket to get the best home pregnancy test, but the result remains a single line. "Maybe the device is just not that accurate," I say. So, I go for a beta blood test and the result is still negative, and I say, "Maybe it is still too early to test it."

Two Worlds: Somewhere Between Illusion and Reality

Can something real be the result of something not real? Can nightmares kill? Can deception rule? Can little lies terminate lives? And for once, can fantasy be real without exception?

Here is an example:

Illusion: Illusion is not real, unless you let it take the reins, then and only then it becomes a part of reality. From what I see, when you respond to a feeling that has been feeding on the roots of illusion it eventually becomes real.

If someone asks you whether pain is real or an illusion, how would you classify it?

I'd say it is a little bit of both. Here's why: Illusion has the ability to make you forlorn and devastated. Consequently, you might shed tears from the pain the illusion caused, and this is my point, the tear drop. Though the cause that led you to shed the tear comes from illusion, that drop will always remain a unique piece of art in the museum of reality.

The essence of our pain might not always be real, but the consequences of our feelings will always be a part of actuality.

My dear child: Know how to distinguish between both worlds and do not get deceived by appearances.

About Time

Time is too fast for those who laugh.
Time is too slow for those who cry.
Time is too long for those who count.
Time is too short for those who regret.
Time is money for those who work.
Time is pain for those who seek revenge.
Time is hope for those who fight and get back up after they fall.
Time is minutes for those who think that the world will end up being a black hole.
But for those who love, time is eternity.
Time is a concept that humans created. Choose the definition that suits you best. Choose the definition that reveals your true identity.

Things You Cannot Escape From

Destiny: You cannot escape from your destiny, because in all ways you are going to have to live it. Your destiny is simply the story of your life.

Fears: You cannot escape from your fears, because they exist in a place you can never hide from. Face them instead.

The End: You cannot escape from the end, because once something has started, it must come to an end.

Birth and Death: Two things you can never run away from, because in this case you don't have a choice. To me birth and death are two brackets. Your life is what lies in between. Make sure that the content between the two brackets reflects an accurate definition of you.

If you do not face what destiny decides to put in your way, you will have to pay a much greater price sometime later. Remember, running away is just a delay, not a delete. In the game of life, there is no fast forward or repeat. Face your destiny, face your fears, and build a life worth living in the time you have on this earth.

The Dawn of Truth

I have learned that no matter what colors I use to draw the pain within, simple or complicated, easy or hard, only mountains and rivers respond, only wind can tell, only birds listen and only time can heal.

Stars were my only witness, and darkness my only companion.

The words of truth written in the sand were the only proof I found, but the rain washed them away.

Proving innocence takes not only time but souls as well.

Know that secrets cannot remain hidden forever. Neither the deepest graves, nor the biggest caves, can hide their light.

There will be a moment, now or later or after I die, when truth will reveal itself and dig its way to the stage of justice, in the middle of the bright daylight or under moonlight.

Every birth witnesses the dawn of a new beginning, a dawn that I shall call truth, when lies and evil burn away, one after another.

The truth is a double-edged sword. One end is knowing how to obtain it and make it work for your own good. The second end is knowing when and how to speak it.

About Options

This is how we humans live.

We have always had and will always have a list of options that form every decision we make in our lives.

You will run out of options only when you stop looking for them.

Never stop looking for them.

When you say, "I don't have any options," you have already made your choice. Because not having a choice is an option itself. Running out of choices is a decision that has already been made earlier and it leads you to a dead end.

Things to Keep in Mind

Each line in this list is the result of a story in my life.
1) When you have a dream, do not waste your time waiting for the perfect moment, because any moment can be the right one.
2) When you get an opportunity, grab it and hold on tight.
3) Your failures make you stronger, motivate you, give your successes a better taste, and make you proud of yourself.
4) Believe in what you want to be and not what you have to be.
5) As long as you live in today, you better do your work today, and don't say there will be time tomorrow. What if tomorrow never comes?
6) Changing people is hard, but changing yourself is harder.
7) If you want to win people's hearts, know what is going on in their minds.
8) If you are looking for happiness, start with your heart and not with your hands.
9) If you want to be successful, you must listen, listen and listen, and then speak. That is how you find

opportunities, and that is why you have two ears and one mouth.
10) Be patient and be wise. This is how you survive in the school of life.
11) Little things can make your life extremely happy. Simplicity is the key.
12) There are so many ways to prove to a person that you love him/her. Saying it, despite the fact that technically it is the easiest way to prove it, can in fact be the hardest way. But nothing exceeds the powerful effect of a true confession.
13) Life always makes sense, and for those who say it does not make sense, change the way you think and things will hopefully start to make sense. Sometimes we just can't grasp the big picture. Pause and have a break, you deserve some rest.
14) We call things complicated not because they are, but because we don't give ourselves the chance to think about the simple threads that have become tangled to make things only seem complicated.
15) The greatest strength comes from the deepest wound.
16) Never look back and ask why. Because the answer is ahead. Be patient, and know that the element of time will always answer your questions. For every "why" there is a simple "because" if you just give it some time.
17) Always hope for the best, pray for the best and expect amazing.
18) If you try everything all at once, you will lose it all

together. Being wise is not trying everything in our lives. Life is too short, so watch, observe and learn from others. This guarantees you wisdom. You don't have to make all the mistakes to learn all the lessons. A smart person learns from his/her mistakes, and a wise person learns from others' lessons as well.

19) No one always wins, and no one always fails. Life is a mixture of both. Each one of them is the result of the other. This is where hope comes from.
20) It is not the wound that hurts, it is the scar it leaves behind that makes humans forever bleed.
21) The right decisions hurt sometimes and make us bleed. Then they heal and set us free.
22) When you have an idea and people keep saying it is impossible, just hide the prefix and get started.
23) Moving on is easy, but what most of us get trapped in is the letting go phase. Remember, the first to forget is the luckiest, and the first to let go is the happiest.
24) Wisdom does not come with age; it comes with what life decides to put you through.
25) Don't overthink, stop worrying, forget about "what if," and put your assumptions aside, because if it is meant to be, it will hopefully be.

The Power of Believing

The power of believing is a precious gift that God has given to you, and being thankful for it is in fact the best way of using it.

In some life circumstances, the power of believing is the only thing we need to pass the tests of reality. Or let me say, the tests of destiny.

Books and movies give one of two answers. It is either yes or no. In life, these answers are not enough to pass these tests.

Follow what you believe is right. Follow what you think makes sense, the right sense for you.

The act of believing is not easy to reach, and it may be difficult to maintain. But once you find your inner peace and have faith in what you do, your soul will reach the highest point of serenity, and nothing in this universe can compete with that. You will find joy in everything you do.

They Always Know

Though sometimes we say things we do not understand, do things we are not certain of, and hear things that make absolutely no sense, this does not change our identity. And those who know us in their hearts will always find the reason, the right reason, to explain our extraordinary behavior.

This is true friendship. A true friend will always know and understand the page you are on even when you are in a different chapter. And a true friend will accept you regardless of your differences. It is the mark of true friendship.

A true friend finds the purpose in your strange behavior, instead of wasting time dwelling on differences.

Friendship is a precious treasure. Be careful in choosing your friends and be wise in maintaining these relationships, because friendships are for life.

The Double F Method

When you face failure in life, remember the Double F Method. The equation is so simple and only two variables are required. Here is how it works:

First, you face the problem, then you get to fix it. Face and fix: the double F. Try the silliest options, too. Sometimes they work very well. Trust me on that one.

Running away from chaos buys you some time. It is a tempting option at difficult moments because it seems to you the perfect solution. This may be true, but only temporarily. Running away has a price that you cannot afford to pay later.

In the end, those failures make you who you are and make you appreciate the life that has been granted to you. So be patient and, more importantly, be thankful. Everything in life happens for a reason.

Trust Your Hidden Power

Batman, Superman, Zorro, Wonder Woman, Powerpuff Girls. They are all heroes. They all have something in common. Muscles? No. These heroes believe in themselves. They believe in their hidden powers, and that is what keeps them going forward. Their faith in their abilities makes them what they are and what they want to be.

There is a sentence I often hear in movies and cartoons that has been engraved in my mind: "You have to believe in your powers if you want to use them." Which means that power is a feeling or a desire that comes from within when it is believed in.

It is true that those heroes have muscles, but muscles need fuel. A strong desire that makes them unique and supernatural individuals with extraordinary abilities, invincible and undefeated. This power is strong belief, combined with a taste of faith, and a twist of pure love on top.

It all started with a desire to change. Batman, Superman, Zorro, Wonder Woman and Powerpuff Girls exist in stories and fantasies, but who made them? We made them, we introduced them to the world, and this makes us the real heroes.

The question is: What stops us from becoming them? The answer is ours to find out.

You are not born a hero. It is something you become.

There, But Not

A star not dimmed by the dawning light that erases the last tinges of darkness.

A soft sound that breaks the murky silence of the night.

The remnants of romance, somewhere between dawn and twilight.

An uncharted spirit, roaming the wild misty shades of a young aurora night.

The scent of an ancient, endearing love that is neither here nor there, yet its stain is everywhere.

A mysterious word combining both warmth and cold. Felt, but never spoken or heard.

A strange desire that comes but never goes.

A captivating stare that changes the concept of time. Intruding, yet strongly familiar. A stare that answers the questions my conscious once asked.

A calming voice calling my name, like a lullaby. Causing a flashback whirling around an indistinct spot, leading to a velvet stupor.

In Her Eyes, I Saw Myself

Once upon a time, above the clouds, somewhere among the pearls of rain drops, and over the arch of a rainbow, we met.

In the ballroom of a Russian castle, surrounded by walls covered in royal red velvet and a magnificent golden ceiling engraved with flowers and vines. The Medieval wooden floor bore witness to the marks that left hundreds of myths behind. The double French doors were carved with faces that told thousands of stories, never one the same. There was a seething mass of guests and faces. Yet some faces are meant to last forever between the lines of memory.

An old man with frizzy grey hair and a thin freckled face was leaning his arched back against one of the marble pillars in the corners. He did not speak or move, but his crinkly dull eyes and sallow wrinkled face spoke hundreds of words, one after the other. The more he gazed at me, the closer I got and the more intrigued I became. Before I realized it, I found myself taking small slow steps towards him until I was standing right in front of him.

Before I could speak a word, I noticed the most beautiful two-year-old girl leaning on the old man's chest, smiling as if she were listening to a magical harmony that allowed her to escape to her own dreamland. The gleam in her eyes was like the luminous dust of a newborn star. Pretty as a picture and pure as driven snow. Her cheeks were soft as clouds and red as beets, and her thin, chestnut brown baby hair moved every time the old man took a breath. She glanced at me for a moment, then tapped on my face with her soft and chubby pink fingers and smiled a smile that added a little bit of magic to a perfect scene.

A moment later, I heard a familiar voice. My husband was calling my name, so I started to quicken my pace to keep track of his voice. Though the ballroom was full to the brim with people, I heard the sound of little footsteps that echoed against the red velvet walls. I turned back, and it was her again. She was running towards me with eyes that could hardly contain the joy. When she reached me, she hugged my legs to ask me to lift her up, which I did, wishing from the bottom of my heart that this perfect moment would last forever. I walked towards the old man to return the little angel, and at the same time I felt a soft hand on my cheeks and a voice asking me to wake up. I woke up and I could still feel her soft fingers resting on the palm of my hands.

If dreaming is what it takes to meet you again, I would sleep my entire life to be with you. Some dreams are meant to be real. Some dreams are worth every risk, beyond the darkest shadows of doubt.

I promise to wake up the next time, holding you in my arms. Will you promise to be there?

He Knows You Can

God puts you through it because He knows you can do it.

If it gets harder ... pray.

If it changes ... adapt.

If it rains today ... there will be beautiful rainbows tomorrow.

Remember: The test of destiny is not about life being fair or unfair. Do not blame it on life, because what you choose to do is enough to determine that principle.

Remember: You do not need sympathy or someone's shoulder to cry on. You can share with someone and pour your feelings out but do not break and allow yourself to get used to it. Because if you do, it will drain you, it will become a deadly addiction.

Remember: Reinforce your faith and do not rely on luck, love or fear. Raise prayers and not complaints.

Remember: Share always and forever, because sharing is caring.

Remember: As long as you can look up to the sky, there will be hope and prayers to be heard. Grace will descend, and wishes will hopefully be attained.

The more faithful you are, the more satisfaction you will get.

Mind Over Material

You do not know who you are destined to meet in life, and who you will choose to be with. You do not know what the circumstances will be. You do not know if your loved ones will be there to protect you and guide you.

There are two kinds of people you will encounter in life. There will be people who care for and value your precious mind and kind heart, who will accept you for who you are. There will be other people who are blind to that and who are driven by material things, superficial in every sense of the word.

Hold on to the ones who cherish your imperfections instead of pointing them out. Hold on to the ones who believe your simplicity is the essence of your beauty. Hold on to the ones who smile always and forever, regardless of the circumstances. Smiling and being nice to people are free of charge. They fix things like magic, better than a fairy's wand.

Stay away from people who focus on your heels and forget how beautiful your eyes are. Stay away from people who classify you based on the clothes you wear. Stay away from those who would not give a single credit to your unique soul to shine and speak of love. We live at a time when clothes and cars are worth much more than kindness and pure hearts.

Love yourself first. Not many will risk their lives to dive into the deep dark ocean to see the secret of your enchanting beauty. But if and when they do, choose them to spend your life with.

"Mind" people will give you what you need. "Material" people will teach you how to use it. Show your worth, and what you are truly made of. You are bulletproof. Titanium.

Be thankful for both kinds of people in your life. Without both, you would not realize which is poison and which is the antidote.

Final Thoughts

I wanted many things in life, and nearly killed myself to achieve them. But if I had known then what I know now, things would have been very different, and much easier on my soul. God always has a better plan. Always and forever. He gave me what I needed when I needed it. And if I had to go back and do things again, I would be more patient and enjoy the time I wasted in agony and fear of the unknown. I would go back to listen to the advice of my parents, because they were, they are, and they always will be, right.

*****

I believed deeply and expected amazing and in the end, I was rewarded, because God gives you according to your beliefs and expectations. So expect great things and reinforce them with honest belief and strong prayers. The choice is yours to make. Start now.

*****

There are limitations to science, and sometimes to our imagination too. There are boundaries to reality and logistical solutions. Yet, prayers, hopes and beliefs are not bound by any kind of restriction or limit. What are you waiting for?

*****

Let no human judge you on the choices you make, simply because no one ever walked your path. Experiences may be similar, yet every human being is different.

*****

Each journey is special and each journey is a work of art. The deeper the content of that piece of art, the more it is worth sacrificing for. And yes, it is worth it.

*****

In this life we live, there is nothing more painful yet more beautiful than the birth of a new life. It is a wonder that cannot be fully explained, or analyzed. It is only felt.

Dear Readers

Happy endings exist at all ages and chapters of life.
They are earned.
Every happy ending involves some kind of journey.
Shove away fear, and believe with all your heart.
Take that first step.

To my beloved precious daughter, Baby Bee:
God willing, one day, when you're old enough to
understand the circumstances of our pregnancy and
your birth, when the time and place are right, this will
be your gift from your father and me.

I hope you like it.